RETURN
PARTY O. NINE:
Life with Sextuplets + One

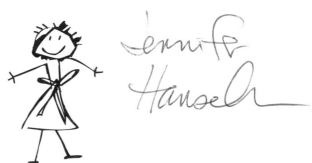

by Jennifer Hanselman

Saddle Point Publishing • Hudson, OH

ISBN 978-0-9800481-0-0
Printed in the United States of America

Cover photograph by The Picture People
Book Design by Sharon Incorvati

Saddle Point Publishing
7947 Valley View Rd.
Hudson, OH 44236
saddlepointpublishing.com
partyofninebook.com

First Edition

*I am honored to dedicate this book to two excellent friends,
Loretta (there'll be no living with her now, Mike!)
and Gayle, with many thanks for your unending
support and love.*

*And also to Keith, for holding my hand
through 12 years of adventures.*

• •

Table of Contents

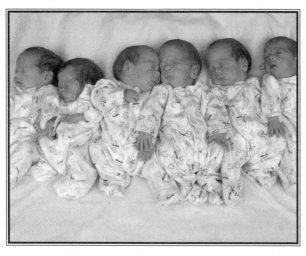

The babies' first photo together at 6 weeks old. Left to right in birth order:
Isabella, Sophia, Kyle, Logan, Alex and Lucy
Photo courtesy of Ted Stevens/Akron Children's Hospital

Introduction

If you're reading this book, chances are good that you already know a little about my family's story. You may even have read my first book, *Party of Nine: The Triumphs and Traumas of Raising Sextuplets + One.* You may have seen us on television or in the newspaper.

What you haven't seen is what's been going on in our crazy life for the past two years. The first book was filled with stories about dealing with babies who grew rapidly into toddlers, and the challenges my husband Keith and I faced in protecting them from themselves. In this installment, our new job is protecting them from each other.

This book is the next two years in the lives of Isabella Jean, Sophia Ivy, Kyle Allen, Logan James, Alex Edwin and Lucy Arlene and their super big brother Connor. The following chapters are filled with month-by-month glimpses of these former toddlers who've now become preschoolers and all their growing pains, strong opinions and struggles for independence (and the best toys, of course). Some chapters have been previously published in local newspapers or magazines, but many are brand new stories that I hope you enjoy reading for the first time.

Before we begin, here's a brief refresher course on how our family went from three people to nine, all in the space of one minute on February 26, 2004: Keith and I struggled to get pregnant and used fertility drugs to conceive Connor, who was born January 14, 2002. Eighteen months later, we used those same drugs to attempt a second pregnancy. On the second try, we found out I was pregnant and said prayers of thanks.

During our first ultrasound at six weeks, those prayers of thanksgiving changed to prayers for strength and courage as we found out I was carrying sextuplets. Against our doctor's advice, we elected not to get rid of any of our fetuses through selective reduction and took a leap of faith in attempting such a high-risk pregnancy.

I spent nearly six weeks in Akron General Hospital at the end of my pregnancy, waiting for the babies to grow enough to survive. At 28½ weeks, the sextuplets were born via c-section just moments apart at 9:42 a.m. All were incredibly tiny but miraculously healthy, with weights ranging from Sophia at 1 pound 9 ounces to Isabella at 2 pounds 10 ounces. Our 14-pound cat Gizmo weighed more than all the babies put together.

After spending nearly two months in the Neonatal Intensive Care Unit at Akron Children's Hospital, we brought the babies home to our tiny, 1,000 square foot ranch and our new lives truly began. At the beginning, we had a fantastic crew of 75+ volunteers who came at all hours of the day and night to help feed and care for our fragile babies. As the kids got bigger and stronger, we moved to a larger house (3,000+ square feet) with a big yard and plenty of room for our growing family to spread out.

And grow they have. We have been so blessed that all of our kids have been incredibly healthy, and we've had nothing more serious to deal with than ear tubes. From the day they were born, we've always known that each of our kids has a very strong, completely unique personality. Those personalities have become much more pronounced as the kids have gotten better at expressing themselves.

Isabella, our first-born sextuplet (and don't you forget it!) is a diva at heart. She has always been very melodramatic, throwing the hugest fits and most teary tantrums, all at the top of her lungs. She loves playing dress-up and can't go to sleep without her ratty brown puppy, pink fleece blanket and the bathroom light on. She's in love with "Jeffy," the teenage son of our friend Loretta.

Sophia, our tiny peanut, uses her size to her advantage and plays the victim to get sympathy. At four years old, she still weighs just under 25 pounds, and that's fully clothed after eating a big lunch. She doesn't let her small size stop her from getting exactly what she wants and she has both grandfathers wrapped around her tiny finger.

Kyle is still sweet, laid-back and very cuddly. He has also been diagnosed with autism (more about that later) and is completely nonverbal at this point. He loves Thomas the Tank Engine in any form (books, movies, scraps of wrapping paper) and frequently strips Alex's bed so he can sit and look at the Thomas sheets. One of his favorite things is a nice, long wagon ride.

Logan is a smiling tough guy who is equally happy wrestling with Alex or singing and dancing along with *High School Musical*. He loves to dish out the rough stuff, but as soon as he gets a push or smack returned, he comes sobbing to me, wailing, "I need a hug! I need a hug!" As you might imagine, he spends a lot of time sniffling on the time-out step asking for a tissue.

Alex has recently had a huge improvement in his speech and talks non-stop about everything. He's a perfectionist that has to have everything just so (he demands the orange cup, yellow bowl and red sippy lid on his juice) and gets very frustrated when I do things my way rather than his. He loves cars, trucks, trains and airplanes.

Lucy is the little mommy of the group. She's concerned about why things happen and how people are feeling and wants to help whenever I'm cooking something. I sometimes have to ask her to stop talking and give my ears a break because her questions are endless. She spends a lot of time making up games with dolls or animals and her bed is always filled with lots of buddies.

Big brother Connor is high-energy and demanding at times. At others, he acts as a third parent, helping his brothers and sisters put on shoes and coats, getting refills for them at mealtimes and sticking on Band-Aids when my hands are too busy to get there. He likes to feel like the boss, and loves reading books and watching movies about pirates, knights and dinosaurs. He plays soccer and has enjoyed his first year of "big kid school."

My husband Keith, my eighth child, is a chemist at a pharmaceutical company. He is a big kid at heart who knows all about toys and has a large action figure collection of his own that he occasionally shares with the kids. I couldn't ask for a better partner in this crazy life since he keeps me laughing and sane throughout the good and bad times.

And then there's me, a former advertising writer turned stay-at-home mom. I find this job to be the most challenging and rewarding one I'll ever have. Although I have seven demanding little bosses, long hours and non-existent pay, I know that what I teach my kids every day can change the world. Each morning, I begin with a prayer for strength and patience!

It is my privilege to share the stories of my Party of Nine with you. I hope they entertain and inspire you and make your life seem a little easier!

• •

Lucy says, "Go potty? No thanks!"

Chapter 1

Feeling the Pain of Potty Training

October 2006

It seems so long ago that I first began this whole potty training odyssey. Now that I'm nearly done, I can honestly say that potty training is one of the absolutely worst things about having kids, but also one of the most rewarding when it's finally finished. I don't mind skipping the diaper aisle at all!

I've been spending a lot more time than I'd like in the bathroom lately. No, I'm not having potty problems. No, I'm not trying to hide from seven kids that insist on screaming my name every 15 seconds. Instead, I have been patiently reading books, blowing bubbles, giving stickers and offering treats, all in a pathetically unsuccessful attempt to potty train the first of my sextuplets.

I began with Lucy because she frequently tells me when her diaper is filled, expresses interest in the potty and is the most talented talker of the bunch. I consulted manuals written by experts, checked out on-line message boards, read countless articles and bought several potty training books and videos. In short, I did not go into this unprepared or ill-informed.

You'd think that having done this once before with my oldest son, Connor, I should have no problem dealing with the latest candidate for potty training. However, Connor was a rare and difficult boy to train and took so long that I began to give up hope he'd ever learn. He was nearly trained by his resourceful babysitter just before he turned two. Then, six little bundles of joy disrupted the whole process and knocked us back six months until we felt ready to try again. It was almost a year and a half from the start of the training until the end when we finally tossed the training pants and went with big boy underwear.

Remembering the long months spent on Connor's training, I was determined that Lucy's should go faster and definitely easier. I prepared an opening day full of fun and games to show her that going on the potty is a wonderful and magical experience. I got a doll that wets to practice with and we went through the day-long routine recommended in one of the books I'd bought, which included skipping Pull-Ups and going directly to underwear. I nearly went insane from concentrating all my mental and physical energy on getting a tiny dribble to end up in the potty chair.

At the end of the day, Lucy had peed once in the potty (probably by sheer coincidence) and had numerous accidents, but I assured myself that we were headed in the right direction. As the days came and went with no sign of success and lots of wet and soiled clothes (and carpets and couches and bedding), I became less sure of what I was doing. I finally abandoned the books, went with my gut and put the Pull-Ups back on.

Those first two weeks, I spent hours every day sitting on the hard tile in our bathroom, exhibiting a strained smile and exaggerated patience as we read book after book. It seemed like after 20 minutes of sitting and waiting, the magical event would happen five minutes after we gave up and returned to the playroom.

And then came that glorious day when Lucy said, "I have to go potty!" and we discovered that for once, she didn't mean "I've already gone potty in my pants!" It seems that all those weeks of practicing had finally begun to sink in, slowly but surely. Hundreds of stickers and tiny cups of treats (and my sore bottom) had been sacrificed on the altar of knowledge, but those dark days faded in memory as the weeks went by with increasing signs of success.

Even big brother Connor stepped into the role of cheerleader, happily hopping up on the big potty to demonstrate while Lucy watched intently from her potty chair. "But don't worry," I heard him tell her while they sat and tried together, "Everyone has accidents. You just tell Mommy and she'll clean it up!"

As she became more confident in her new skills, Lucy began demanding to go to the potty every 15 minutes or so, just to get out of the gated playroom. Her sisters caught on to the magic words and also started yelling, "I go potty! Mommy! Pottttteeeeee!"

After a long and trying day of asking to go, but not producing much, Lucy told me again that she had to go right after supper. I didn't really believe her, so I put her on the potty and told her to call me when she was done, then returned to sweeping the kitchen floor. When she called me a few minutes later and told me she'd pooped, I still didn't believe her, until I rounded the corner and saw the evidence for myself. In my entire life, I've never been excited to walk into a stinky bathroom until that moment!

We did the happy potty dance together and I heaped praise on her until her eyes shone and she couldn't stop grinning. After getting the sticker and double treat she had worked hard to earn, she charged into the playroom and began bragging about her accomplishment and her rewards.

I've often said that I wished kids came with a port in their heads, so we could just download new data into their brains when it was time to learn a new skill. Still, there is something satisfying about working so hard to teach a child something and seeing that "Aha!" moment when it finally clicks and they get it. I know we have a long, looooonnng road ahead before we're free of potty chairs and training pants, but I'm confident we'll get there, one smelly success at a time.

Connor

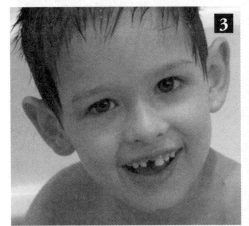

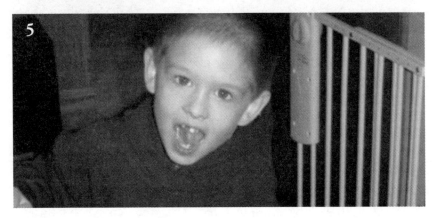

1: Connor's pumpkin, Halloween 2006
2: Suited up as a Power Ranger, February 2008
3: What a ham! February 2007
4: Happy to be taking a train ride. March 2007
5: Doing the Wild Connor Dance, November 2006

Connor

6: At the Cleveland Metroparks Zoo, March 2007
7: Seriously into Play-Doh time. June 2007
8: Ready to fight a dragon! September 2007
9: "Please?! Can I keep him?" September 2007
10: The soccer star is ready for his first season. September 2007

Logan is a cute and flat M&M.

Chapter 2

Obsess Much?

November 2006
Previously published in the *Beacon Journal*

I love my husband dearly, but Halloween always strains my patience with him. Keith gets just like a little kid around the big day and it's my job to rein him in and remind him that preschoolers don't want to wear helmets to look like an army of Storm Troopers. I doubt we'll ever have a simple ghost or witch costume in our house if Keith has anything to do with it.

I used to snicker quietly at my parents' and parent-in-laws' obsession with the weather. It seemed any time we visited with either set, the weather was an ever-present subject of discussion, complete with multiple viewings of the Weather Channel to catch the latest updates. "Borrrring!" I used to say to myself with a mental eye-roll.

Last week, however, I discovered one more piece of evidence that I am slowly but surely turning into my parents. In the days leading up to our annual outings to Boo at the Zoo and neighborhood trick-or-treating, I was plastered to the Weather Channel myself, watching storms roll across the area. When the "Local on the 8s" just didn't get there quickly enough for me, I resorted to the Weather Channel website, which offers hour-by-hour forecasts and instantly updated radar for obsessive mothers like me.

This year was the first real trick-or-treat experience for my two-year-old sextuplets, and I was dreading the thought of fighting with umbrellas or mittens in addition to treat bags and unwieldy costumes. Every check of the forecast left me more and more pessimistic about the chances of a break in the storms so my little ones could enjoy Halloween festivities.

Up until Thursday morning, we were still preparing for raincoats and umbrellas as part of our Halloween costumes for that night's Boo at the Zoo. However, mere hours before we were set to leave, God smiled on us and the heavens finally stopped dripping.

You may remember my story of last year's Halloween debacle where we made our triplet strollers into train cars, much to the disgust of the passengers who took turns staging fits throughout our entire time at the zoo. This year, my slightly crazy husband was bound and determined to turn the strollers into pirate ships, complete with rigging, masts, cannons, creepy music and even EYE PATCHES for the little pirates. After telling him he was out of his landlubbin' mind and threatening to make him walk the plank, I came up with a more pleasant alternative.

A few yards of brightly-colored felt glued onto circles of foam board turned into some pretty cute M&M's costumes, which the little ones tolerated surprisingly well. Big brother Connor had wanted to be

Superman since the first Halloween costume catalog arrived in July, so he strutted around the zoo parking lot twirling his cape and striking heroic poses while our posse of adults tucked the rest of the kids into wagons.

I am happy to report that this year's zoo trip was much more pleasant than last year's visit (which is no reflection on the zoo, but rather on my kids' tempers). Instead of screaming the entire time, Alex yelled, "Wheeee!" and clapped his hands while Kyle giggled at him in their shared wagon. The girls amused themselves by walking on all the curbs like balance beams. Connor led the charge to each new treat station and Logan stretched out flat in his wagon, looking remarkably like an M&M someone had stepped on.

The girls spent the entire drive to the zoo talking about waking up the animals, so they were a little disgusted to find the tiger unwilling to wake up for their shrill little yells. However, all was quickly forgiven when they picked out little tiger toys in the gift shop and pranced out to the van roaring and giggling.

Just as we completed our zoo adventure and got everyone buckled into the van, the rain began again, leaving us to heave a sigh of relief and offer up a silent prayer of thanks for the excellent timing.

After another day of obsessing over the radar, Saturday arrived with some really freaky weather. We went from rain to blinding sunshine to pea-sized hail to snow to thunder and lightning and back to sunshine in a matter of hours. I kept one eye glued suspiciously to the window while my mother-in-law's suggestion of indoor trick-or-treating kept sounding better by the second.

Keith also caught the forecast fever and kept up a running commentary with five-minute weather checks from the computer. "There's going to be a break around five or six o'clock," he reported optimistically as the rain gusted down in sheets and slammed sticks and leaves against the windows.

Sure enough, the radar was right and the skies cleared just in time for trick-or-treating. We got everyone stuffed into shoes, winter coats and slightly bedraggled costumes and headed out for a second round of Halloween fun.

The girls loved seeing the neighborhood dogs, and the boys giggled as the wagons rolled over bumps in the sidewalk while we went from house to house. Once Alex got a piece of candy in each hand, he was satisfied to skip the rest of the houses and happily watched the girls march up and down the sidewalks saying "Tank you!" as candy landed in their bags. After 15 minutes, the wind started getting the best of us, so we headed home just ahead of a few raindrops.

Now, in the wake of the Halloween festivities, I am left with a sugar hangover, two extra pounds and a pointless desire to constantly check on the weather, even though we have no outdoor activities planned for a while. The leaves do need raked, though, and you have to have good weather for a few days to dry them out properly, so I guess I can rationalize a few more visits to weather.com, right? Maybe I'll just eat a little more of my kids' chocolate while I check, for energy of course.

• •

Alex

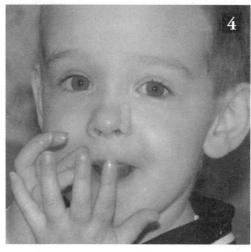

1: Laughing it up, February 2007
2: Trying out a new bike, March 2007
3: So intense! February 2007
4: Macaroni, the latest fashion accessory! May 2007
5: Giving the big boy bed a test bounce, September 2007

Alex

6: Silly face, January 2008
7: Can you tell he loves cameras? October 2007
8: Ready for trick-or-treat, Halloween 2007
9: "I'm going to get Mommy for printing this!" March 2008
10: Putting on a festive face for Halloween, October 2007

"Here's what I think of my glasses!" says Kyle.

Chapter 3

Thumbs Down for Glasses

December 2006

The first year with Kyle's glasses was a partial success. They were on more than off, but we spent a lot of time going back and forth to the optician's office for replacements. I think the final total was five or six pairs in a year. The second year, we got a new pair that fit him a little better. He broke the first set in less than 16 hours and has refused to wear the replacements ever since. They are still in pristine shape, sitting on a shelf waiting for Kyle to be ready to try again.

I have always hated to see wee little kids with glasses. I'm not sure why it bothers me so much, and Keith makes fun of me for it, but I always feel a little sad for them. Part of the problem is that I remember my own childhood spent in glasses. Although I didn't get them until third grade, I can remember as early as first grade needing to sit in the front row so I could see. I don't remember hating glasses so much as just being annoyed by them. They were constantly smudged or sliding down my nose or getting scratched (and then I was in trouble).

Since Keith also had glasses in elementary school, I knew it was only a matter of time before our kids needed them because of our bad eyeball genes. I didn't quite expect that the first pair would be before their third birthday.

I took the kids to their eye doctor for a routine check-up last month. We've known since they were born that because they were so premature, they were at increased risk for eye issues. They have had regular checks since being in the NICU, so I didn't expect anything unusual this time around.

Alex and Logan were pretty cooperative about looking into the machine while the nurse took pictures of their eyes and pronounced them healthy. Kyle, who hates to be forced to hold still for any reason, flopped and kicked and screamed when it was his turn. It took me and two nurses to hold him still for a moment, and it took the doctor about 15 seconds to see that Kyle would need glasses. Of all the kids it could've been, it had to be Kyle, the least tolerant of anything new!

After another 15 minutes of screaming and holding tightly, we had a prescription and headed off to the optician to pick out tiny little glasses. We ended up settling on a pair that wrapped around his ears, since those were one of the few pairs small enough for Kyle. We waited the required two weeks, picked up the glasses and then the fun really began. Luckily, I had bought the breakage protection plan…

Kyle wouldn't really try on the glasses for the fitting, so we just did the best we could. He refused to wear the glasses in the car, so at home I put him on my lap, wrapped my legs around his body to hold his arms down and hooked the glasses onto his ears. After a few minutes of struggling, I finally let his hands loose and he fidgeted with the glasses and then left them alone. For about five minutes. The rest of that day, I kept inding them on the floor, or seeing a sibling trying them on, but he gradually adjusted.

On the second day, Kyle quickly discovered that the plastic-coated arms of his glasses made great chewy toys. In a matter of minutes, he had the arms so shredded that he couldn't wear the glasses because they felt scratchy on his ears. We toughed it out for two more days before I finally gave in and called the optician for another pair. She assured me that I was not the record holder for shortest amount of time between pairs, which made me feel slightly better.

For the second pair, we added a stretchy strap to make it harder for Kyle to yank the glasses off. At least then when he flipped them off, they just dropped down around his neck and weren't found lying all over the floor getting stepped on by the rest of the herd.

Unfortunately, that second pair didn't last long either (less than a month), and now we're onto our third pair. At this rate, we'll have a new pair every month, and I'm so thankful that I bought that breakage plan!

Kyle seems to be doing a little better with tolerating the glasses now, and his brothers and sisters happily rat him out when he's messing with them or getting ready to chew on them. Still, I have a feeling that we're not quite finished with the glasses war just yet.

I still feel a bit sad when I see Kyle wearing his glasses. I just don't like them, even though he looks very cute and sort of like a little thumb-sucking professor with them on.

In typical fashion, the girls were angels at their own eye doctor appointment, and the nurses and I all breathed a collective sigh of relief when they sat like little ladies with no fussing and let their eyes be pronounced okay for a year. The doctor says Lucy may need glasses in a year or two, but she'll be as easy as pie after the riots we've had over Kyle's glasses.

Since having the sextuplets, I've grown to appreciate the truth of the old saying, "What doesn't kill you makes you stronger," so I think I'm broken in and ready for future eye adventures. I probably shouldn't say that, since seven kids can always come up with new ways to torment me. My eyes hurt just thinking about it.

• •

Alex is lookin' good in his Christmas vest and matching purse he swiped from his sisters.

Chapter 4

Minor Christmas Miracles

January 2007
Previously published in the *Beacon Journal*

I love Christmas, but I often have to fight with my attitude around that time of year. I tend to get overly focused on all the extra things that need doing, rather than the moments I might be missing with the kids. I always end up paying attention to the right things, but sometimes not until the very last minute.

You hear a lot about big miracles during the Christmas season—a divine conception, a heavenly babe, angels in sheep pastures and a guiding star. Sometimes the stories of big miracles are so spectacular that we forget about all the little miracles that still happen in our lives every day. Experiencing another Christmas with my sextuplets and their big brother proved to me that there are lots of small daily miracles waiting to be discovered if you just take a minute to see and celebrate them.

I was in typical high gear until December 23: making cookies, wrapping presents, doing last-minute shopping and trying to preserve my sanity while keeping up with the extra work and the usual daily chores created by a family of nine. When the morning of Christmas Eve arrived along with the start of my second migraine in 24 hours, I was as grouchy as the proverbial bear and badly in need of an attitude adjustment.

I said a little prayer for strength, made a pact with my sourpuss husband for both of us to try not to be so grumpy, and kicked off the day by changing our countdown sign to "1 day 'til Christmas." We got the kids up and moving and ready for breakfast, and as we all sat down to eat together, I noticed miracle number one: no one was sick! Last Christmas was a blur of stomach ailments and disgusting messes to clean up, so we figured we had nowhere to go but up this year. We chalked it up to divine intervention that this holiday's bodily messes were confined to runny noses. I was delighted to merely wipe a few noses as I remembered how rotten we'd all felt a year earlier.

As we got the kids dressed for church in their matching red Christmas outfits, I had to remind myself what a miracle it was that they were all strong and healthy enough to wrestle with me as I shoved arms into sleeves and folded cuffs on festive socks. Three years ago, it was only Connor I was dressing while heavily pregnant with the sextuplets and praying hard for a very large miracle.

After marching proudly into church in their cute new clothes, all seven kids loved watching the choir perform "Drummer Boy," complete with an actual drummer. Connor stood up on the pew to see better and the rest looked on in open-mouthed amazement. After church, we made lunchtime a bit easier with take-out from McDonald's, where we got the sextuplets their first ever Happy Meals. Until then, they'd always had to share large boxes of nuggets and fries that we doled out in handfuls. They were delighted to discover their own miracle: fries come with TOYS? How cool is that!

We returned to a very warm church service in the evening, where Connor was excited to sing with the kids' choir. He'd practiced his favorite part of the song ("Glo-ho-ho-ho-horia!") over and over again, and sang that like a champ. It was the rest of the song that eluded him, so he spent the time wiping his nose on his arm and turning around to watch the bigger kids singing behind him. Still, for those few miraculous moments, his face was cherubic as he sang with his mouth formed into an "o" and it was easy to forget that he'd been bouncing off the walls and getting on my nerves all afternoon.

The final song, "Silent Night," was sung by candlelight, which provided another miracle by turning six pink-cheeked, sweaty, tired toddlers into a half-dozen angels with light reflected in their eyes. As I watched them solemnly stare at the candles and listen to the quiet singing, I had my annual "Aha!" moment that always reminds me why I do all those crazy things to try to give my kids the best Christmas possible.

Christmas morning arrived and seven kids tumbled down the stairs and eagerly dove into the stockings that Santa had left on their chairs at the kitchen table. In our house, Santa brings breakfast in the stockings, which is mostly junky stuff I won't let them eat the rest of the year, so they're happy to sit down and have their special treats before tearing into presents. (Getting seven kids trained to willingly eat breakfast before opening gifts is a rather large miracle in itself!)

During the gift-opening frenzy, guardian angels had to be watching over five crazed adults who managed to avoid hand injuries while frantically snipping, clipping and gouging at toy packages with scissors, wire cutters and pocket knives. I swear that toy manufacturers must give bonuses to their employees based on the number of wire ties they can attach to a single toy. Does one Dora the Explorer doll really need 10 wire ties for the body and another dozen to attach all the accessories to the package? At the end of the day, we had produced an awe-inspiring 12 bags of trash, one of which could easily have been filled with just wire ties.

The afternoon was relatively quiet, with kids playing contentedly with new toys. A bonus miracle was a reduction in fighting as the kids actually—gasp!—SHARED their new toys and traded with each other without the usual amount of screaming and shoving.

And so the year ended on a good note, with all of us anticipating celebrating many more miracles and milestones as Connor turns five in a few weeks and the sextuplets look forward to their third birthday in February. I am waiting for a little miracle of my own: quiet time, when the six-pack starts going to preschool four mornings a week in March.

Hallelujah!

• •

Isabella makes a few calls before getting on with her day.

Chapter 5

A Day in My Life

January 2007
Previously published in *Akron Life and Leisure*

When I was asked to write this article, I had to first introduce our family for readers who may have missed the beginning of our story. On the day I describe, it was a challenge to make myself stop every few minutes and write things down. When the piece was finished, I felt tired just reading it!

If someone had told me when I was 20 that I would have seven children before I was 30, I would have suggested they seek professional help. And yet here I am, the mother of Ohio's first set of sextuplets, who turn three at the end of February, and their big brother, who just turned five this month. God sure does have a strange sense of humor, as my husband Keith likes to say!

It was a rocky, bumpy road to get pregnant with Connor, our first baby. We tried lots of painful and expensive fertility treatments to conceive and loved him to pieces when he was born. Eighteen months later, we decided to try the same expensive treatments again, and got our money's worth in a big way when I got pregnant with sextuplets.

After a difficult and very high-risk pregnancy, Alex, Logan, Kyle, Lucy, Sophia and Isabella were born three months early. We practically lived at Akron Children's Hospital for the next two months until the kids grew strong enough to come home.

Since then, life has been organized chaos, with two very busy parents trying to keep afloat. We decided early on that the best way to survive was just to tackle one day at a time with a sense of humor. One recent Monday, my longest and toughest day of the week, I wrote down every crazy minute to give you a glimpse of what it's like to be a mom of seven. Could you keep up with me?

6:10 a.m.
Roll out of bed and stagger into exercise clothes after hitting snooze alarm three times.

6:15
30 minutes on the treadmill watching world tragedies on CNN Headline News wakes me up and makes me realize my life could be harder.

6:45
Drag myself upstairs to coax Connor out of bed. We grab clothes and take them downstairs to dress.

7:00

Keith and Connor leave for work and preschool. I feed four cats and one goldfish and head off for a shower.

8:00

After a quick breakfast while checking emails, I start the first of many loads of laundry and make my to-do list. I hear the first thumps of little feet hitting the floor upstairs and say a quick prayer for strength as I start the day.

8:15

The girls are enthusiastically up and racing around their room. In the next room, the boys are burying their heads under blankets and wishing for 15 more minutes. We all head for the stairs and I end up carrying four of the six down, two at a time. Who needs weight training when I've got 30-pound toddlers?

8:20

Potty time for Lucy, who screams, "Help! Help!" as I carry her to the bathroom while the others begin dumping bins of toys in the playroom. Once at the potty, it's "No, no, no!" as I unzip her footie pajamas and take off her soaked Pull-Up.

8:22

Leave Lucy wailing on the potty to do her business, and come back to the play room in time to see that Isabella has found stickers under the couch and is sticking them all over the windows. First mess of the day!

8:23

Pull stickers off windows, then change Kyle and Logan's diapers.

8:28

"I pee!" Lucy calls from the bathroom, and she has—in the potty chair, on the bathroom floor and all over her pajamas. Clean up the various puddles and run upstairs again for dry clothes.

8:40

Finally get around to changing Sophie, Alex and Isabella. Sophie starts the first brawl of the day and ends up in the time-out playpen in the kitchen.

8:50

Two of my occasional volunteers arrive to help out for the morning. They walk in to see Sophie wailing in the playpen, Kyle crying at the gate for his breakfast and the other four fighting over toys in the playroom.

8:59

Cups of milk and bowls of cereal are ready, so I open the gate and let the kids out into the kitchen. They immediately go in six different directions to find something to destroy before they're captured and buckled into their booster seats.

9:03

Hand out vitamins, everyone counting and yelling "Yay!" when we're done.

9:05

The ladies refill cereal bowls as I empty the dishwasher.

9:20

Forgot to take off Kyle's glasses. He smears the lenses with banana goo and smashed cereal while I'm not looking.

9:27

The kids are still eating as though they haven't been fed in a week. I've folded two loads of laundry left over from yesterday and put load number two in the washer.

9:35

The kids finally finish eating and are ready to be wiped off (or hosed off, in Kyle's case). Once clean, they go back to the playroom, where the girls promptly strip down to their diapers and run around giggling.

9:45

Six chairs and bibs are wiped and a small mountain of cereal is swept up from the floor. I head upstairs to pick out clothes for the day and straighten the kids' rooms.

9:55

With one arm full of clothes and the other full of toys retrieved from under beds, I return to the playroom. The ladies and I each grab a screaming, protesting toddler and wrestle an outfit on them.

10:05

Six kids are dressed and the adults are all out of breath. I sit on the floor with Kyle, wrap my legs around his torso and pin his arms to his body so I can shove his glasses on without him ripping them right off again. The glasses are a new addition, and he's destroyed the first pair in three days, so the replacements are being closely guarded and fastened on with a strap.

10:15

After reading a few books and starting a "Bob the Builder" DVD, I leave the ladies in charge of the playroom and start cleaning. Today is sheet washing day, so I strip and remake the boys' cribs (what a pain), remake the guest bed and put away three baskets of laundry.

11:00

Put load number three into washing machine and vacuum all upstairs bedrooms except Connor's. The floor of his room is littered with Lego's and pirate ship pieces, and I don't want to be responsible for sucking up some important sail in the vacuum cleaner. (It's happened before and the results are UGLY.)

11:15
Take Lucy to the potty again, but I've remembered too late and she's already wet. Sigh.

11:20
Run out to garage and hold breath while dragging overflowing trash can and recycling to curb for tomorrow's pick-up.

11:30
The ladies do the diaper changes while I start lunch and Kyle begins his pre-meal windup by whining at the gate again.

11:50
Lunch is ready and Kyle has finished his lunch preparations by yanking off his glasses.

Noon
The kids are eating and a few moments of blissful silence descend upon the house. I put the breakfast dishes into the dishwasher, start laundry load number three and give the mail a glance in between circling the table with seconds of macaroni.

12:15 p.m.
Kids are wiped and herded up the stairs to bed. They scatter once they hit the upstairs landing—some go to Connor's room to grab his toys, one slams the bathroom door, some go to their own beds and some get in bed with a sibling and try to hide under the covers.

12:20
Kitchen clean-up begins. It's not easy to sweep up macaroni and cheese, especially when I've stepped on it and smashed it into the tile. The ladies flee to the quiet of their own homes.

12:35
The girls are running races and giggling like maniacs, so I sit with them to make sure they stay in their big-girl beds. The boys are still in their cribs and show no signs of wanting to get out, thank goodness.

1:00
The girls are finally passed out on their faces, but I hear Kyle still jumping in his crib. He has a dirty diaper, so we go downstairs, change it and come right back up, much to his disgust. He howls for a few minutes, then gives it up and goes to sleep.

1:10
Lunch and time for a chapter or two of a new library book for me.

1:20
Lunch comes to an abrupt end as I am eating an apple and notice a funny smell on my hand, which turns out to be a missed chunk of poo under a fingernail. Suddenly the apple isn't too appealing.

1:30
Lunch dishes to dishwasher and start it up so we'll have some clean sippy cups for supper.

1:40
Fold and put away two loads of laundry and remake my bed with clean sheets.

2:05
Check emails, pay some bills and balance the checkbook. Consider starting to drink, but realize there's no money left to buy alcohol.

2:50
Alex, Sophie and Lucy are up again and Lucy yells, "Mom! Mom! MOOOOMMMMM!" loudly until I bring them down to the playroom. Alex hasn't slept after all, which means he'll be a royal pain tonight.

2:52
Change Lucy's poopy Pull-Up and put her on the potty to remind her where messes are supposed to go.

2:54
While Lucy's practicing, I pour juice cups, then return and read her a book while keeping an ear on the playroom.

3:07
We return to the playroom and Sophie says, "Hi Lucy! You pee?" Lucy says, "Nope!" and they skip off to play with animals in the corner.

3:17
Logan is up and creating a green cloud in the boys' room, so I change him and give him some juice.

3:22
I play, wrestle and read a few books. Playtime for me is way too short!

3:52
It's Logan's turn to pick a movie, so he picks "Thomas the Tank Engine," much to the disgust of the girls.

4:00
Isabella and Kyle are still sawing logs, but I scrape them out of bed and make them come downstairs so they'll sleep tonight. They're not happy about this.

4:05
Keith calls to say he's leaving work and is on his way to pick up Connor.

4:10
Strip the girls' beds and throw their bedding in the washer.

4:15
Referee a few playroom fights and make a few phone calls.

4:35

Change Isabella, Sophie, Kyle & Alex's diapers, all of which are dirty.

4:45

Toss a giant bag of stinky trash out on side porch.

4:50

Keith and Connor arrive home and I get one of Connor's flying attack hugs as he jumps on me and shoves his pile of artwork in my face. I hang the new masterpieces on the art wall in the kitchen. Keith gives me a quick kiss, waves to the kids and ducks into the bedroom to change before rolling up his sleeves and diving into the chaos.

5:00

Field a phone call from my book publisher about media inquiries while getting out ingredients for supper.

5:08

Start supper and feed pets.

5:15

Empty dishwasher and set out plates for our assembly-line supper.

5:18

Keith pours cups of milk while I put the girls' sheets in the dryer.

5:25

Supper is ready and doled out onto nine plates. We open the playroom gate and unleash the hungry horde. All seven are eventually confined to their seats and we go around and around the table, handing out plates and silverware and refills as the gobbling begins. In between, Keith and I grab a few bites from our own plates before jumping up to get something else or retrieve a dropped sippy cup.

5:55

Dinner's done (or thrown on the floor) and clean-up begins again.

5:58

Lucy taken to potty, where she manages to pee just in the potty and get a treat as a reward.

6:30

Finished the kitchen and more laundry, so I'm off to make up the girls' beds.

6:45

Bath time! The kids love baths and fight over who gets to go first and stay in longest. We do this assembly-line style, like everything else, and just rotate all seven kids through the same tub of water. By the end, both Keith and I are soaked to the skin and the bathroom floor is a lake.

7:15

Baths are done and all seven kids are zipped into clean footie pajamas. We take all the towels and clothes to the washer, which is now groaning and smoking after a day of constant work.

7:20

I take the girls' blankets up and make sure everything is ready for the stampede upstairs.

7:25

Bedtime for the sextuplets. We brush six sets of teeth and pin the girls' pajama zippers so they can't take them off and run around naked (they can accomplish this in about 12 seconds if we forget the pins). Lights out and a big sigh of relief from two tired parents!

7:35

It's a goldfish crisis! Nemo, Connor's goldfish, has decided to float upside down or sideways since supper. Keith mentally prepares his speech to Connor about why Nemo went to fishy heaven. (As of press time, that silly fish is still swimming funny and showing no signs of expiring any time soon. Even the pets go a little crazy in our house!)

7:40

Make the menus for the week and prepare shopping list and coupons for a quick grocery store sprint after Connor gets to bed.

7:45

Chill with Connor for a few minutes and watch a little Scooby Doo until bedtime.

8:00

Hustle Connor upstairs and do the allergy medicine/teeth brushing/story routine, then run back downstairs to shove shoes on and grab shopping list.

8:25

In the car and on my way to the library to exchange the kids' weekly movie stash.

8:50

Arrive at BJ's and dash quickly through aisles, grabbing nine gallons of milk, a jumbo box of diapers, a three-pound box of hot dogs and a trunk full of other giant-sized essentials for the week.

9:20

Arrive at Acme and pick up the rest of the shopping list, hurrying to beat the store closing announcement.

9:55

Slide out the doors just before they kick me out, load the back seat full of bags and drive wearily home.

10:10
We've unloaded the overflowing car and begun to put things away.

10:30
Keith vacuums the playroom while I scoop some low-fat ice cream for us.

10:40
We watch a little television, eat our ice cream and poke each other when we begin to nod.

11:15
I do what Keith calls my "security sweep." I check each child and adjust their blankets, then check all doors and flip on alarm before brushing my teeth and collapsing into bed.

11:30
Lights out for Mom and Dad. Only a few short hours until the whole routine starts again!

"This is only temporary," Keith and I remind ourselves during tantrums, sickness or difficult childhood phases. We try not to think about driver's education, prom dresses, braces, dating or college and only look ahead a few weeks. One big event on our horizon is preschool in March for our six-pack. I am looking forward to four mornings a week of quiet time to get my house in order and do a little uninterrupted writing. The kids will get to learn lots of new things and play with children they aren't related to.

In spite of all the busy days, both good and bad, I wouldn't change a thing about my life. We have never regretted our decision to go ahead with our high-risk pregnancy, and our biggest hardship is that there aren't enough hours in the day to spend as much time with each child as we'd like. With a lot of prayers and a truckload of patience, we're making it, one very long day at a time!

• •

Isabella

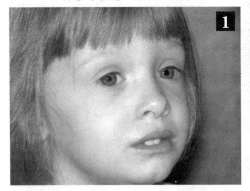

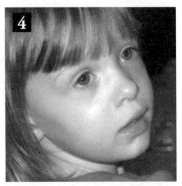

1: Worried Isabella, May 2007
2: Do you like my new haircut? April 2007
3: Getting up close with a museum display, October 2007
4: Future model? February 2007
5: Isabella, right before the big leaf mold allergy attack! October 2007

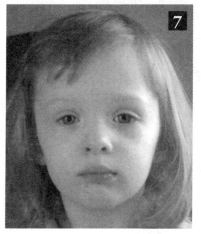

Isabella

6: Mommy and Bella taking a train ride, March 2007
7: "You can take my picture, but you can't make me smile!" November 2006
8: Movie star glamour for Easter, 2008
9: Decorating the Christmas tree, December 2007
10: Yelling at the big fish at the Cleveland Metroparks Zoo, March 2007

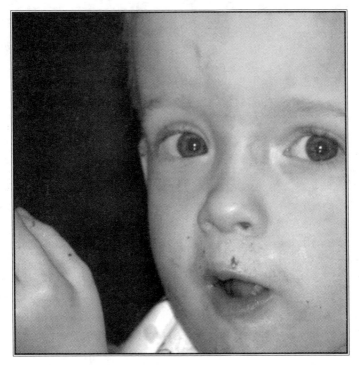

Logan thinks eating like a big kid is messy but fun.

Chapter 6

Big Kid Day

February 2007

Even after more than four years of inevitable change, the kids and I still find comfort in our daily routine. I'm not sure which of us hates a new routine more, but in the end they're always glad to become a little more independent and I'm usually happy to hand over a new responsibility to my "big kids."

I came to the realization the other day that I'm a complete slacker about teaching my kids things. Ever since they were born, I've dragged my feet when it's time for them to learn something new and become a little more independent. With seven young kids, it's just so much easier for me to do things myself with little mess and fuss, rather than stand back and bite my lip while I watch my children struggle to do something all by themselves.

Changes are always painful in our house because we're so rigidly routine-oriented out of necessity. If we don't do things in the same order every time, we end up leaving the house without diaper bags or keys or someone's favorite blanket. But at some point, I just have to suck it up and live with the change for a few days until it becomes the new routine.

With the sextuplets' third birthday and the start of preschool right around the corner, I decided to take a look at all our normal routines and see if there weren't a few changes I could make to get the kids to be more helpful around the house and a bit more independent in caring for themselves. Sounds like a dream, I know.

So I started Big Kid Day with what I thought would be a simple change: making them walk down the stairs by themselves after their good morning hug and kiss. I had been carrying them, two at a time, down the stairs and depositing them in the playroom, then going back up twice more until everyone was down. This worked just fine when they were smaller, but now that they're getting to be heavier by the second, my poor arms can barely make it to the bottom of the steps before someone has to get down or get dropped.

I really tried to sell it to them by saying what an exciting day this would be when they learned to be big kids and do some things for themselves. They seemed okay with that idea, until they realized they would be required to actually do some work. It took us 15 minutes and a lot of pep talks before they all made it to the bottom of the stairs under their own power, and most of them had several wailing, sobbing meltdowns in the process.

The next battle was in the bathroom. I made each of the potty-trainee girls walk into the bathroom by themselves, pull their own pants down and up, wipe their own bottoms, flush the toilet and wash and dry their hands. Again, fifteen minutes of wailing and carrying on from Isabella and Sophie, but Lucy was surprisingly enthusiastic about the whole thing.

As they watched me prepare breakfast, all six kids started making protest noises when I pulled out new plastic cups with no tops instead of their much-loved, spill-proof sippy cups. I prepared myself for the spilling extravaganza that was sure to come, and only poured an inch of milk into each cup to start with.

I coaxed six suspicious kids into their booster seats, put their cups within reach and stood back to watch. I gave them another pep talk, and as soon as the first ones tried and inevitably spilled, I said cheerfully, "That's okay! Everyone spills when they're learning!"

After hearing my speech a few times, Logan, who happily spilled more than he got in his mouth, would chirp, "Dat's okay! Dat's okay!" with each new puddle. Kyle promptly drowned his food and his lap just for fun. Isabella took the daintiest of sips and managed to spill very little. Alex and Sophie were willing to try, but needed my help every time. Good-natured Lucy surprised me by flatly refusing to have anything to do with these strange new cups and demanding a "baby cup." By the end of the meal, my cheerful manner was a bit strained and we'd gone through half a roll of paper towels.

Mercifully, even the most challenging meals always come to an end. I announced that I wanted them to ask to be excused, carry their own bowls and cups to the sink and hand them to me. This time, Lucy was much more enthusiastic after watching her sisters march carefully over to the sink and get praised for helping. She finally couldn't wait a minute longer and yelled, "My turn to be big helper!" The boys all needed help to get their things to the sink, and we spilled quite a bit on the way.

At this point, it was already 10:30 and I was exhausted from the strain of doing everything so slowly with a forced smile plastered on my face. I'd lost track of how many times I'd said, "That's exciting!" when telling the kids what they'd learn next.

When it was time to get dressed, I told them I'd like to see how they did getting dressed on their own. I passed out the outfits and the screaming began, so I started helping them one by one. Several of them helped pull shirts over their heads, all of them managed the sleeves by themselves, a few could pull up pants, but the socks were a complete fiasco. Time check: 11:15, the latest we'd ever finished dressing, and almost time to start lunch prep. Sigh.

When I began working on lunch, 12 curious eyes watched me from the playroom. When I got out another stack of new cups, Isabella let out a belly laugh and said, "That's exciting!" in a perfect imitation of my well-worn phrase. Lucy made faces and said, "I don't like them!"

The lunchtime cups went a little more smoothly than breakfast had, so once they'd mastered the basics, the naughtiness began. Logan decided just to dump his cup over and over for fun. Isabella dropped fish crackers into her cup and scooped them out to eat once they got soggy. Lucy again refused to even try the new cup.

By suppertime, the kids were all exhausted from a full day of trying to learn a new routine. I was mentally fried and wishing for bedtime at 4:00. When Keith and Connor hit the door at 5:00, I told them the results of my grand experiment and Keith had to gush over each one trying so hard to be a big kid.

I expected that supper would be a little easier than lunch, but I think we'd all just had enough and the spilling was non-stop. The big helpers weren't so helpful at clearing the table, but Connor jumped right in and rinsed everyone's dishes with enthusiasm and lots of puddles on the floor.

At the end of the day, I had to call the whole thing a good beginning. Lucy had learned to do the whole potty routine herself, including putting on a dry Pull-Up when needed. She still hated the new cups, but I was determined to break her down the next day. (It actually took three more days and nerves of steel to keep me from backing down, but finally a very parched little girl gave it up and started drinking on her own out of a big cup.)

As with any changes in our routine, the first week was the roughest, and then the kids seemed to settle into their new responsibilities and stopped fighting me quite so much. They have unwillingly graduated to Big Kid status, and I can quit saying, "That's exciting!" until the next unpleasant change has to be made. Thank goodness! So much forced smiling was making my face hurt.

• •

Lucy

1: Playtime, February 2007
2: Enjoying an early spring, March 2007
3: Determined to play with all her new toys at once, Christmas Day 2007
4: Just sleeping, or crushed by a giant book? March 2007
5: Cute enough to eat! Halloween 2006

Lucy

6: Making friends at the Cleveland Metroparks Zoo, August 2007
7: Making a fashion statement, November 2007
8: Girls can be knights, too! September 2007
9: Playing with Grandpa Bud's squirrel collection, August 2007
10: This girl's obsessed with rocks, even on vacation in Cincinnati! October 2007

43

"Oh, how I love preschool!" says Sophie.

Chapter 7

Preschool Pandemonium

March 2007
Previously published in the *Beacon Journal*

The kids are now in their final year of preschool, and I still love the four mornings of peace and quiet every week. Although they love their teachers and classmates, they have begun talking about going to Connor's "big kid school" for kindergarten next year, which makes me feel ancient just thinking about it.

For the last few weeks, people have been telling me how sad I would be on the first day my newly-minted three-year-old sextuplets went off to preschool. I kept thinking they were right, imagining myself choking back tears as I dropped them off at school. I figured they might have a problem with me leaving them with strangers, in spite of how anxious they appeared to be to skip off to school like their big brother, Connor. Boy was I wrong on both counts.

After a weekend of non-stop birthday celebrations, I had a few quiet minutes in the kids' rooms Sunday night to pack their pink and blue puppy backpacks with extra clothes and other school essentials. As I thought about the big transition coming up the following morning, an unpleasant thought suddenly hit me like a rock to the forehead.

No, it wasn't the realization that they were starting school; it was the idea that they were suddenly three. That made ME older, too. I didn't sign up for that! Overnight, I had turned into the mother of seven preschoolers, which made me feel incredibly old for some strange reason.

I struggled with that thought all evening and had trouble falling asleep, as did my husband Keith. He was as wound up as a kid on Christmas Eve, but I lay awake imagining that my joints were creaking.

Monday morning came far too early and the kids were less than happy to be rolled out of bed at 7 a.m. instead of their customary 8:15. After the usual grumbling, attempts at sitting on the potty for the girls and diaper changes for the boys, they came to breakfast. They looked as dazed as I felt, and just picked at their favorite Dora the Explorer cereal without actually eating much of it.

After a mostly ceremonial breakfast, Keith and I started getting six reluctant little scholars dressed for school, brushing hair and tying laces on new shoes. To add to the festivities, Connor was home and wanted to see the kids' new school before getting dropped off a little late at his own preschool. In typical 5-year-old fashion, he raced excitedly around, crashing into things and starting fights with his sisters before getting banished from the playroom.

As the time ticked down towards departure, the noise level steadily increased until I was suddenly looking forward to kicking—er, dropping—them off at the curb and speeding away merrily. In our eagerness to get to it, we arrived at school way too early and had to circle the block a few times until a spot at the curb opened up for our monster van to pull in.

A herd of teachers and assistants met us and helped the kids into school, while Connor trotted along with them and Keith and I staggered along in their wake with our hands full of backpacks, diapers, wipes and assorted paperwork.

Once we hit the doors, the kids scattered with their respective teachers and we off-loaded all our cargo into six little lockers and went to say our good-byes. Since we were on a tight schedule to get Connor to school and Keith to a doctor's appointment, I had very little time to feel bad about leaving my kids for their first day.

The only parting tears came from Sophie, who was last seen sobbing in her new teacher's arms, yelling for me as the door closed behind us. (I found out later that the tears dried up in less than two minutes. What an actress!) Kyle hugged my legs and had to be pried off, but the other four quickly found new toys to play with, and waved away my kisses with gestures of impatience.

After all the business of the morning was accomplished, Keith and I celebrated the first day of school with a late breakfast at Bob Evans. We weren't surprised to find that we had no energy left for talking, so we chewed quietly together and tried to ignore an unappetizing conversation two ladies were having nearby about their latest mole removals.

All too soon, it was time to head back to the preschool to see how our new students had fared on their first day. As we pulled into the driveway, we saw six familiar little people heading right for us. Each of them had a puppy pack on their backs, and their faces were filled with the joy of newly-discovered independence as they marched along in pairs with their teachers.

I actually did feel a little sadness then as I watched them come toward us. They looked so grown up that it almost brought a lump to my throat. I might have gotten a little teary if my knees hadn't suddenly started creaking with increasing age as I got out to greet them.

After hearing all the teachers' reports, the first day was deemed a smashing success. All six of them participated in activities, explored their classrooms and shared birthday treats with their new classmates.

Alex actually fussed a little when he had to get in the van, and Logan was nearly inconsolable about a new book he'd had to leave behind.

We picked up a special lunch at the Burger King drive-through and looked at their artwork at the kitchen table while they munched and tried to tell us about their adventures. All six were more than happy to go upstairs for a nap after a tiring morning of learning.

After a few days at the new school, my mini age crisis has mostly passed, and the kids are settling nicely into their new routine. Even our four cats are adjusting happily to four quiet mornings a week. One of them celebrated the first day of school by barfing up a brightly-colored pile of curly ribbon at the foot of our bed. I just sighed and tried to ignore my creaking knees as I bent to clean it up.

• •

Sophie

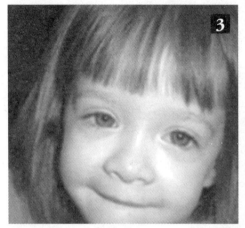

1: *Too cute for bedtime! November 2006*
2: *Cruising on the deck, March 2007*
3: *Being silly, November 2006*
4: *Enjoying Christmas candles, December 2007*
5: *Playing with giant animals at her 4th birthday party, February 2008*

Sophie

6: Buttering up Santa, December 2007
7: Sweet and sassy! Easter 2008
8: Queen for a day, April 2007
9: Having a tea party at the Curious Kids' Museum in St. Joseph, MI, June 2007
10: Picking the perfect baby pumpkins on a school field trip, October 2007

Connor picks flowers for Mommy in our yard.

Chapter 8

So Much for Mommy's Wish List

May 2007
Previously published in the *Beacon Journal*

The kids are now old enough to start bringing home hand-print art from preschool or cute poems illustrated with their own drawings to celebrate Mother's Day. I carefully save all these offerings just to remind myself some day that they really were so little, since the days and years go by much more quickly than I could ever have imagined.

As a mom of seven kids under the age of 6, most days are noisy, chaotic and full of interesting messes, and Mother's Day was no exception. I am an optimistic person, so I started dropping hints to my family on Saturday night how I expected to be treated the following day: no noise before 7 a.m., no bickering, no screaming when I say it's time to go potty and no fighting me to get dressed. And above all, BE NICE TO MOMMY. As you might imagine, I didn't quite get everything I wanted.

The morning started with the girls ignoring my first request by having a big noisy fight over a toy in their room before 6:30. Usually on the weekends, we don't hear them until after 8, so I guess they were just excited about Mother's Day. They followed this with some more screaming as they pinched each other's fingers in the attic door while playing hide and seek.

Not long after that, five-year-old Connor stomped down the stairs and invaded our bed (my side only, as usual), stealing my blankets and pillow and demanding I get up, fix him breakfast and restart the movie he'd been watching the night before. My husband, Keith, reluctantly agreed to take over these duties since it was Mother's Day, giving me about 15 more minutes of sleep before the alarm went off and was beaten into silence.

After a quick shower, it was time to drag everyone downstairs. Since the girls had been awake for a while, they had found the energy to fight me every step of the way to the bathroom, killing a second Mother's Day request. The boys merely grumbled their way downstairs after I'd scraped them out of bed, but began fighting over toys and books as soon as they were fully awake. So much for one more item on the list.

They all managed to keep things to a dull roar at breakfast, then Grandma and Grandpa arrived to go to church with us and the fighting over getting dressed began. While one child was forced to put down a book or toy to get their shirt wrestled onto wiggly arms, a second child would sneak up and steal that book or toy just to hear the first one scream. Sigh…there went another request up in smoke.

After breakfast, I celebrated in my own way by splashing grease on the front of a new shirt I'd just gotten the day before as I put the ham in the oven. I decided I would just have to enjoy the good moments as they happened, like any other day, and try not to expect any special treatment.

With this new philosophy in mind, we rolled noisily into church, where I savored the peace and quiet after the kids went to downstairs to the nursery. I appreciated the colorful carnations each mother was given at the end of the service. I laughed as I shared a piece of cake with Logan and watched him practically unhinge his jaw like a snake to cram a large bite in his mouth. I tried to enjoy the lovely Mother's Day card Connor had painted in Children's Church, while wondering if the still-wet purple paint would wash out of my third shirt of the day (and his own shirt, I later discovered).

I tried to maintain my peaceful state when we arrived home, even after my husband got it in his 33-year-old head to play tag like a kid and accidentally slid through the yard on his knees in his dress pants. I quietly shook my head and tried not to snicker as I handed him the bottle of stain pre-treater while he limped into the bedroom to change. (It only took three washings to get the grass stains out of the knees and seat of his pants. The purple paint mostly came out of the two church shirts, and the ham grease gave it up after the third attempt, too, so it was a good laundry day.)

My mother-in-law was kind enough to bring all the lunch and supper fixings, so cooking was one responsibility I was happy to give up for the day. And when the kids went down for their nap, we enjoyed a little flower shopping in the sunshine.

Just Connor was awake when we got home, so we had a little quality time while he helped me plant a few planters. When that was done, we got out the sidewalk chalk and drew our own flowers on the driveway. The rest of the kids joined us for some playtime in the sun and the boys blew bubbles while the girls admired the new flowers. Kyle, always slow to wake up, was content to sit and snuggle in my lap while Daddy and Connor raced remote-control cars in the driveway and the rest of the kids ran after them, giggling madly.

As I watched seven happy, healthy kids playing and jumping and making lots of noise, I once more counted my blessings. Not a day goes by where my kids don't annoy the heck out of me, but there's always at least one quiet moment of joy, wedged in between laundry, messes, potty accidents, fights and tantrums. That single moment of joy is just enough to keep me going and make me glad to be the mother of seven wild and crazy little kids. Someday when they're old enough to have their own children who drive them nuts, I will have my sweet revenge for all the torments I have endured. But for now, it is enough to have that one moment every day, especially on Mother's Day.

Isabella hangs on the infamous playroom gate.

Chapter 9

Farewell, Dear Gate!

June 2007

Yes, I still have the gate in the basement, more than a year after the infamous day it came down for good. It's like a member of the family, and I just can't bear to get rid of it. It's got tape, crayon and stickers all over it, and couldn't possibly be any good after all the beatings it took, but I still just can't carry it to the curb yet. Silly, I know!

There are some moments so historic that you will always remember exactly where you were when you heard about or witnessed them. These moments become etched into your memory so that whenever someone asks you about that day, you immediately remember your thoughts and feelings so vividly that it's just like living the event all over again.

One of those too-painful-to-forget days for me was The Day the Gate Dropped. (Yes, it deserves to be capitalized just like that!) The infamous gate is the one that separated the playroom from the kitchen and kept all my little savages enclosed when needed so that I could cook in peace and be sure they weren't tearing up the rest of the house when my back was turned. It was a wonderful gate. I loved that gate.

For almost two years, the gate stood sturdy and amazingly unchallenged by my growing sextuplets. It was a pressure-mounted walk-through gate with sturdy but unremarkable white metal bars, but to me it was beautiful in its simplicity. It had a tough-to-manage foot pedal that only Connor and adults were heavy enough to press, so the rest of them were stuck inside whenever I closed the gate.

Sounds like prison, you say? Not so much. My kids are used to boundaries and gates, so to them, it was no punishment to play with their dozens of toys in a large, bright playroom that overlooks our back yard. Trust me, they managed quite a lot of mayhem in spite of my best efforts to make the room a kid-proofed zone.

But like all good things, the gate's time of usefulness had come to an end. With active potty-training in full swing, it was hard for the kids to get to the bathroom on time while the gate was closed, so I decided it was time to take the gate out of the way in the interests of potty independence.

But I really loved that gate, so I kept putting off the big day. Finally Keith told me to suck it up and just do it already, which I thought was big talk from a guy who goes to work all day and doesn't have to deal with the mayhem of seven kids enjoying their newfound freedom.

I picked a Tuesday to go gateless, and then chickened out since I was the only one there that morning. Wednesday, June 6, 2007 dawned bright and sunny, I had two of my occasional volunteer helpers visiting for the morning and I knew it was the day. So I held my breath and yanked the gate out quickly like you'd pull a Band-Aid off a hairy arm really fast to reduce the pain. I really loved that gate, so it was hard to say good-bye to such a cherished and useful friend.

I had a sickening, sinking feeling in my stomach as I put my beloved gate in the basement and squared my shoulders against the chaos ahead. I got the kids out of their rooms and they trooped downstairs, unaware that this was a momentous day. They walked right through the doorway without even noticing at first that the gate was gone. Isabella was the first to see its absence and stood hesitantly in the gap, her heels on the playroom carpet and her toes just touching the kitchen tile while she looked over her shoulder at me, waiting to get scolded.

I sighed and explained why the gate was gone and how I expected them to go right to the potty now when they needed to instead of waiting for me to ask them or having an accident. The girls all seemed enthusiastic about the idea, and then all seven kids set out to test out their new boundaries.

With the gate gone, they now had access to all the bedrooms upstairs, the kitchen, the laundry room and their bathroom as well as the boring old playroom that suddenly seemed much too confining. We still had gates keeping them away from the basement stairs and out of Mommy and Daddy's room at the front of the house, but suddenly a whole new world had opened up to my explorers, and they were determined to wring every drop of naughtiness out of the occasion.

One of the first discoveries was the water cooler in the kitchen. It had a child lock on the hot water tap, but not the cold, so the boys quickly made a game of running by the cooler and swatting at the cold tap to make just a little water run out into the tray. Soon the tray was full, and then it was fun to splash in the lake that grew quickly at the base of the cooler.

When they got in trouble for this game, everyone but Kyle ran screaming in circles around the kitchen table and island. The sound of bare feet slapping merrily on the tile echoed throughout the house as they squealed and slid around the turns, sometimes crashing into chairs or walls. In the meantime, Kyle took advantage of my distracted state to stand on tiptoes, pull the dirty dishrag off the sink and creep away to a quiet corner to gnaw happily on the corner of it. When he tired of that, he pulled all the kitchen towels down and threw them on the floor, which added new, slippery obstacles to the mad race around the kitchen.

The kids packed all of this fun into the first 15 minutes of being downstairs. I thought maybe breakfast would calm them down, but they raced through the meal just so they could get down and start tearing around again. After breakfast, they discovered the shoe and coat closet and spent a few happy minutes trying on all the shoes and shutting each other up in the closet, before I found out what they were doing and put a child-proof knob cover on the door.

The volunteers arrived to a wild, screaming scene (and the kids weren't the only ones screaming, I have to say), and probably wanted to run screaming themselves. One dear woman who hadn't been over in a while asked, "Is it always like this?"

The rest of the morning was spent trying to keep the kids from destroying the whole house. They knocked pictures off the walls and sent them crashing down the stairs, and then figured out the piano lock and beat out some sour notes on the keys. The cats were sulking because I'd had to move their food from the kitchen to the basement to keep little hands from sampling out of the bowls.

We'd also put latches on all the cupboards and drawers, so every time I went to get something out, I'd forget the latch was there, yank it out an inch, crash it into the stopper, mutter a nasty word and release the latch to get a knife. Kyle figured out how much fun it was to bang the cupboard doors open an inch and slam them shut (crash-slam-crash-slam-crash-slam) until I lost my mind and started yelling.

Overall, that's my impression of the entire day: a whole lotta screaming. By the time Keith came home at 5:00, I was ready to run out of the driveway and never come back, but he said he'd tackle me before I got off the porch, so I decided I might as well stay.

After supper, we tried out our wimpy new plastic push gate that was supposed to keep the kids in the playroom long enough for us to sweep up the mess on the floor. The problem was that the gate had to be a few inches off the ground to hit the flat spots on the door posts, so the kids just crawled right under the gate and ran amok again.

The one bright shining moment in the whole day was Lucy actually going to the potty and peeing by herself without any prompting from me, so at least the idea for getting rid of the gate seemed sound.

It took quite a few days for the novelty of going gate-less to wear off, and it took me a few days more to get used to cooking with kids under-foot. Like any other change in our routine, it's been painful but necessary, and just one more sign that my kids are growing up too quickly to suit me.

Now and then, I still go to the basement to visit my gate and think fondly of those days of confinement. I really did love that gate.

• •

Lucy splashes Kyle, while Isabella wades
in the lake on vacation.

Chapter 10

Conquering the First Vacation

June 2007
Previously published in the *Beacon Journal*

Although it's a ton of work to go on vacation, it's still worth it to us because it gives us time to enjoy our kids and just be a "normal" family for a short while. We save our pennies all year long to afford that one week every summer where we get to go away and have fun as a family. Even though we're really just moving the work load to a new location, I know the kids will look back with happy memories of our summer trips together.

I survived our first ever family vacation! I feel like Rocky, jumping up and down at the top of that long, exhausting flight of steps, hands in the air in triumph. Okay, so my abs and right hook aren't anywhere near as good as Rocky's, but I still think it's a tremendous achievement to pack up and relocate six three-year-olds and a five-year-old for eight days and seven nights away from home.

Being the over-planner that I am, I started researching a lake shore vacation to St. Joseph, Michigan, reserved an economical rental house and began a packing list last August, which drew snorts of disgust from my husband. I talked my parents into going with us to help with the kids, fully aware that none of us might be speaking by the end of the week. As the time drew closer, the packing list became a novel, and it might have been shorter to list the things we didn't need to take, rather than those we did.

The week before vacation, we started counting down with the kids and talking about going to the beach and all the other fun things we had planned. The morning of departure, our house was in super-hyperactive mode, with seven kids running and screaming and four adults trying to avoid stepping on little toes while loading the last of the supplies into the van.

Finally, with a hearty shove, the last box was crammed in, the little ones were strapped into their seats and we rolled out of the driveway with kids shouting "Bye house!" "Bye cats!" "Bye flowers!" "Bye swords!" (This one was from big brother Connor, who was mildly disgusted that we made him leave his pirate swords at home.) We were off on a five hour drive to southwest Michigan, with high hopes for good weather and minimal tantrums.

The kids did amazingly well on that long ride, nearly three times as long as any we'd ever attempted before. We timed our departure so that most of the ride was during afternoon nap time, so it was mercifully quiet for at least two hours of boring turnpike driving. On the second half of the drive, we had to dig into the snack and bribery bag a few times to hand out treats for distraction, but we arrived at the little vacation house just before supper with most of our sanity intact.

The kids ran screaming (yes, this is a daily activity, no matter where we are) from one room to the next, while my mother and I frantically collected breakable knick-knacks and stored them in a bedroom closet for safe-keeping. The kids were banging in and out of bedrooms, picking places to sleep and slamming each others' fingers in doors. I foolishly thought I could prop the worst door open to keep the injuries to a minimum, but our little 22-pound Sophie forced the door shut against the prop and ripped the door right off its hinges. (Luckily, it was easily fixed with longer screws and a tube of white model paint to cover up the shiny screw heads and fresh splinters of wood around the hinge.)

Once our mountain of junk was unloaded, we ate a quick supper and stuffed the kids into the wagons to walk the five blocks to Lake Michigan, thinking we'd just enjoy the view and come back for swimming in the morning. The kids foiled that plan by jumping right into the 60-degree lake with all their clothes on!

After a long, tiring day, the kids finally crashed in their strange beds and the adults finished unpacking before dragging off to bed, hoping for a chance to sleep in a little bit in the morning. No chance of that! Connor was up and racing at 6:15, and the rest of the kids soon followed, so we were all up, dressed, full of breakfast and down at the nearly-deserted beach by 9. The water was chilly, but the kids splashed around in it, built sand castles and picked up dozens of mussel shells. It was a picture-perfect morning with soft sand, beautiful sunshine and water so clear and blue you could barely tell where the lake ended and the cloudless sky began.

And so the days rolled by quickly, filled with daily trips to the beach, picnics, long walks and time to relax and read books in the evenings after the exhausted kids finally dropped off to sleep. We spent a lot of time walking through picturesque downtown St. Joseph and admiring their outdoor art installations, one of which was a series of 30 miniature fiberglass cars decorated by local artists, just the right size for kids to climb on. Another favorite activity was the Curious Kids' Museum, which was filled with dinosaurs, blocks, an apple orchard, a farm with working water pump, science experiments and play areas ranging in theme from a jungle to a Japanese tea room to a kid-sized Coast Guard boat.

We took a day trip to Chicago to the Shedd Aquarium, where the kids' favorite part was the baby beluga whale named Bella. Our own Isabella, who weighed 2 pounds 10 ounces at birth, was amazed to hear that Bella the whale was 125 pounds as a newborn. Another road trip was to the Potawatomi Zoo in South Bend, Indiana, where we rode a little train and watched a very large tiger stare into the faces of the kids as he paced by the glass. On our drives, Alex was our water watcher and would yell, "Osha!" (for "ocean") whenever we passed a river, lake or large puddle.

By the end of the week, we'd eaten ice cream and "junky food" (as Connor called it) at every local shop, tracked sand into every room and every bed of the rental house, gotten fried in the sun that shone every single day and pronounced our first family vacation a big success. When Sunday morning rolled around, we were tired but happy, and crammed our gear back into the van for the long trip home.

As we got set to cruise out of town, I said a silent prayer of thanks for surviving and enjoying the trip beyond any of my expectations. Miraculously, we'd had no injuries that a Band-Aid couldn't fix, no property damage we couldn't repair and the adults were still smiling more than snarling. I eased the van out of the cramped driveway for the last time and said, "Bye, beach house!" The kids responded by singing out, "Bye ocean!" "Bye sand!" "Bye Curious Kids' Museum!" "Bye little cars!" "Bye ice cream store!" And the list continued, long after we'd left town with our heads full of happy thoughts of home.

• •

Keith blows bubbles on the deck
for the kids to chase.

Chapter 11

And Now, a Word from Daddy

June 2007
Previously published in the *Beacon Journal*

Keith was terrified when he was asked to write a brief Father's Day column for the newspaper about his unusual family. He reluctantly agreed, as long as I consented to fix up his spelling and grammar issues before he sent it in. This chapter is the final result of that collaboration.

As I look back on my sixth Father's Day, the fourth as the father of sextuplets, I find that each one gets a little more rewarding, a little more challenging, and a lot more enjoyable. One of my favorite things to do is watch seven little people exploring outside.

I love seeing them learn to climb up the ladder to go down the sliding board, and Kyle, our newest climber, practically runs up the ladder now. After I showed them how to do it a few times, Sophie, Isabella, Lucy and Logan no longer need me to place their feet on the footholds of the climbing wall. On a recent trip to the backyard, Connor was excited to show me the old bird's nest that we had discovered together last summer. It's great to watch some of the kids move on from baby swings to big kid swings and hear them scream "Higher!" (or as Alex says it, "Iher!") as I'm pushing them.

Father's Day is also a time that I see my dad laughing hysterically as I pull my hair out over something the kids have done. He just sits back and says, "I remember a time when another little boy did something like that." It's scary to see how my kids are so much like me. For example, Connor will try any tactic in the book to get me to buy a toy for him. It's no longer just directly asking for a toy, but composing the question so that the only answer can be "Yes." (He's going to make a good lawyer some day!)

It's really funny watching the younger kids as they raid Connor's room and come out swinging his pirate swords and Star Wars light saber. Now I think I'm going to have to hit Connor up for some pointers on how to convince Mommy to get seven more light sabers, six for my little Jedi and one for me, of course!

My friends with older kids always joke with about what I'll do when my kids are old enough to drive, date, get braces, go to college, etc. I try to brush them off and say that I just take it one day at a time, secretly knowing that I'll want a Schwarzenegger Terminator robot to answer the door to scare any little punk that wants to take out one of my princesses.

As far as driving goes, I don't even want to think of that and I definitely don't want to think of seven little cell phone bills. I do have lots of things to look forward to showing them in the future, like their first roller coaster ride, first time swimming and first time riding a bike without training wheels.

This is a great journey, and I'm enjoying it (almost) every day!

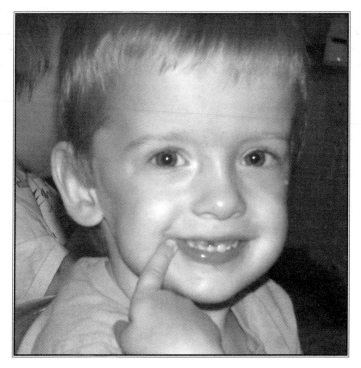

Logan shows off his new and improved smile
after losing his first tooth.

Chapter 12

Tale of the Tooth

August 2007

*Logan's such a tough guy that I'm amazed he's only knocked out
one of his own teeth. He loves to wrestle, push and shove,
and frequently needs a visit from the "Boo Boo Bunny"
(our rabbit-shaped ice pack that gets a lot of use)
to take the swelling out of the latest bump on his head.*

I've always thought it was incredibly cute to see kids with their first
teeth out, smiling that gap-toothed grin, so proud to be a big kid at last.
However, when that jack-o-lantern grin belongs to a 3-year-old, it seems
a little unfair that they should ruin the pretty smile they worked so hard
to push out such a short time ago.

Logan has always been my tough boy. He loves to wrestle and is the
one frequently sitting on the time-out step for pushing and hitting. He
can do the naughtiest things while grinning at me like he's the cutest
thing ever. (Okay, so he is cute, but I'm pretty sure he's got horns hiding
under that blond hair.) So I guess I shouldn't have been surprised at all
that he was the first one to start knocking out his own teeth. Perhaps it's
a minor miracle that he didn't knock anyone else's out while he was at it.

The whole mess started with a bath. We were on a family trip to
Chicago and he fell in the hotel bathtub and hit his mouth on the edge.
I didn't think much of it once we got the bleeding stopped, but noticed
one of the teeth had a rough edge to it the next day.

When we got home, I took him to the dentist and they x-rayed it
to make sure the root was okay. (That was a real ball of fun, keeping a
3-year-old still enough for an x-ray when he's pitching a fit about the
piece of plastic in his mouth!) The tooth didn't seem wiggly, so we
decided just to keep an eye on it.

A few days later, my mom was up for a visit and we got out some
fold-up nylon play tunnels for the kids to muck around in. I left and
went to run some errands with Connor and was in the middle of a craft
store when I got a frantic phone call from Mom. "Logan just knocked out
his own front tooth!" she said. "He was in the tunnels and started crying
and came out with a mouth full of blood! It looks like it came out whole.
I've washed it and put it in a bag, and he's stopped crying now and doesn't
seem to care."

My first thought was, "He's ruined his cute little devilish smile. Let's
shove it back in!" but I called the dentist to see what to do. They said to
bring him and the tooth in. Again.

Hoping for a dental miracle, I rushed home, grabbed Logan, and dashed out again with Connor in tow for "moral support." Connor spent the ride to the dentist giving Logan a gory blow-by-blow account of how he'd lost his own front tooth in a preschool swing incident and had to go to sleep while the doctor cut the root out. Good thing Logan couldn't really understand much of what Connor was telling him, or we'd have been at a grade-one meltdown by the time we hit the dentist's waiting room.

Logan pranced in like he owned the place, marched back to the exam room and hopped right up in the chair like an old pro. He gladly let the dentist examine his bloody gums, and seemed proud of his handiwork when the bagged tooth was passed around for review. Dashing all my hopes, the dentist said that they're not in the habit of jamming a front tooth back in, so we'd just have to adjust to Logan's new look since it would be that way for years until his permanent teeth started growing in. He did say that Logan had done a top-notch job removing the tooth all in one piece, so at least surgery wouldn't be required to remove any leftover bits.

Logan adjusted very quickly to the idea of having only one front tooth on top. He spent a quick moment admiring his tough new smile in the bathroom mirror, then hurried off to stir up his usual trouble and never fussed about the tooth again.

It took me a while longer and many long glances at the shark-like tooth we'd tried to save before two thoughts hit me: "What the heck does the Tooth Fairy bring a kid with no concept of what money is for? And where do we put the tooth if there's no pillow?"

Logan still sleeps in a crib, so in the end we decided the Tooth Fairy would find the tooth just fine if we put it on the floor under his crib. The next morning, a very wise Tooth Fairy had skipped the money and left a toy car shaped like a shark with large, gold front teeth, which suited Logan just fine.

I thought the tale of the terrible tooth was concluded, but two weeks went by and I noticed that his gums kept on being red and puffy, and the other front tooth started to turn the same shade of gray that Connor's had right before it was pulled. This meant (you guessed it!) one more trip to the dentist and yet another x-ray to make sure that the tooth wasn't cracked below the gum line. The dentist gave the okay and told me to check Logan's gums every day for an abscess until the swelling stopped.

As we were heading for the exit, I was thinking gratefully that it would be a sweet long time before I had to come back again, until the hygienist cheerfully called after me, "You know, it is about time to schedule Logan for a first cleaning! Did you want to set that up today?" "Love to!" I said through my own gritted teeth. Logan just smiled his devilish smile and I could swear I saw those horns even more clearly as I reached for my calendar.

• •

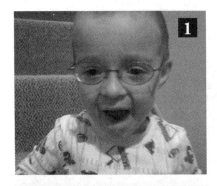
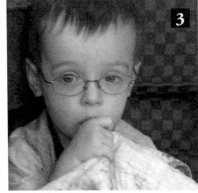
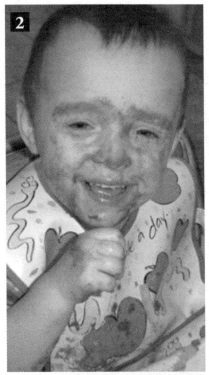

Kyle

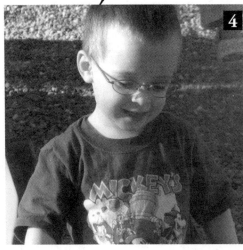

1: *"Hey! It's almost Christmas!" November 2007*
2: *This boy REALLY loves baked beans! November 2006*
3: *Thumb and blankie: an unbeatable combination! March 2007*
4: *Sliding makes me smile! April 2007*
5: *Enjoying the fresh air, March 2007*

Kyle

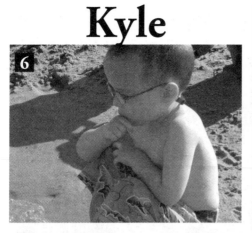

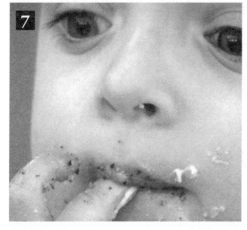

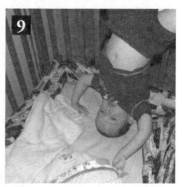

6: *Studying the waves in St. Joseph, MI, June 2007*
7: *Savoring every crumb, February 2007*
8: *The many faces of Kyle, October 2007*
9: *Looking at the world from a new perspective, September 2007*
10: *Mommy's little stinker, Halloween 2007*

*Connor is all ready
for his first day of kindergarten.*

Chapter 13

Butterfly Beginnings

September 2007
Previously published in the *Beacon Journal*

On Connor's first day of kindergarten, I experienced a foretaste of the teen years to come. We bickered quietly all through the parking lot as he frantically tried to get away from his two embarrassing parents and march into school like a big boy who didn't need any help. I know it's only a short step to the eye rolling and sighs of exasperation that come with the teenage years.

Back in the dark ages when I was in school myself, the end of summer used to inspire a mixture of excitement, dread and anticipation at the thought of buying new boxes of sharp crayons and shockingly clean sneakers. As the school bus rolled up on each first day, all those feelings seemed to jam together in my stomach like one huge ball of spastic butterflies, all trying to fly away up my throat and bring my breakfast with them.

I had a reoccurrence of those same old feelings last week while getting my kids delivered to their schools on their own first days. It was silly, really, I told myself on Tuesday morning. I wasn't the one starting kindergarten, like my oldest son, Connor, but still I was incredibly nervous for him.

We had visited his new classroom and met his teacher the day before, so he was sure he knew right where he was going. As we fought first-day traffic, unloaded his supplies and headed for the door, he complained loudly at being walked into school like a baby by both of his parents. He had no way of knowing that it was not the carefree kindergartener that needed help finding the way on that first day, but rather his two dumbstruck parents, who were both trying to figure out how we suddenly got old enough to have a student in elementary school.

Connor, a beanpole since birth, was nearly a head taller than many of the first- and second-graders that he passed as he marched confidently toward his new classroom. He had rehearsed the route to me over and over ("I go straight down the hall, past the picture of Harry Potter, down the stairs and look for the monkey on the door and that's my room!") and followed it without a misstep.

When we reached the fabled monkey, he was all set to charge into class and join the circle around his new teacher without so much as a backward glance at the loving parents that had prepared him for 5½ long years for this moment of independence. With a sigh of exasperation and an eye-roll worthy of a teenager, he consented to pose for a photo and give us the briefest of hugs before leaping away to begin his new adventure.

And just like that, Keith and I stood there alone in the hallway. We felt bad for maybe ten seconds, which was about the amount of time it took us to get lost on our way out to the parking lot without our little navigator. We had no time to wallow in our feelings of old age, or sniffle about our baby boy growing up because we had six more eager students waiting at home for their own preschool open house later that morning.

As the sextuplets geared up to greet old and new teachers, Keith and I tried to pace ourselves for the strain of transporting six kids' worth of school supplies from the curb to the classroom. When I received the preschool supply list early in the summer, it didn't look too bad at first glance. A parent with one child could manage with a backpack and a few plastic bags. Our stash filled the cargo area of our 15-passenger van, piled level with the top of the seats.

At the appointed hour, we jammed six kids, two grandparents and two parents into the front of the van and set out. Unloading the kids was the easy part. Less simple was figuring out how much we could carry in one trip while still keeping the kids from running amok. Keith pulled an overflowing wagon and tugged on a reluctant Kyle, while I balanced boxes and grasped little hands as we staggered along behind two grandparents who were trying to keep their charges from running flat-out for the door.

The kids had a great time getting reacquainted with their favorite classroom toys from last spring, while their teachers marveled over how much they had grown and changed during the summer. Keith brought another wagon load from the van and I began distributing our boxes up and down the hallway and tucking supplies into lockers. When it was time to go, there was much weeping and wailing when we forced the kids to put down the toys they'd scattered in three different classrooms.

After depositing the six-pack and two tired grandparents at home, Keith and I went back for our big kindergarten boy. Connor came charging out the door with a huge smile on his face and nothing but happy things to say about his first day. In fact, I don't think he ran out of steam for at least 10 minutes. At lunch, when Grandpa tried to get him to talk about kindergarten, Connor sighed and said, "You tell him what I said, Mom. I'm too tired!"

That night, I packed six little puppy backpacks with changes of clothes and reviewed my mental checklist of where everyone had to be and at what time. After a restless night, where I woke often to check that I hadn't overslept, morning finally arrived along with an even larger flock of stomach butterflies. I needn't have worried; my mother and I had seven kids fed, dressed and ready in enough time to clean up the kitchen, start laundry and still have 15 minutes of nervous thumb twiddling until it was time to get in the van.

Connor had wrung a promise out of me that he was to be allowed to go into school all by himself, after repeatedly chanting the route to his classroom. When I let him out at the curb and he marched up the sidewalk and disappeared inside like a seasoned pro, my mother and I exchanged glances as if to say, "Is he five or 15?"

The preschool drop-off didn't go so smoothly, as Kyle had a crying fit before the van even stopped moving. Logan waited for his moment until he was out on the sidewalk, then he collapsed and wailed with his mouth open wide enough to show off the gap where he'd knocked out his front tooth several weeks ago. After a little more sniffling (and not even from me or Grandma), all six shouldered their backpacks and trotted off for the beginning of another year.

At home, Mom and I kept saying things like, "Is it only 9:45?" or, "I hope those girls aren't having accidents in their big-girl underwear right now." After several minutes of deafening silence, I happily said good-bye to my stomach butterflies until the start of the next school year, and settled down to enjoy my first morning of peace and quiet in three months. God bless teachers everywhere!

• •

Logan

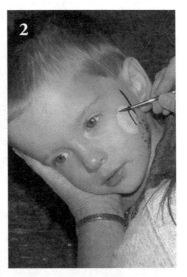

1: *They all fight over this bike, and Logan's happy to be the winner for the moment! March 2007*
2: *Getting painted for Halloween, October 2007*
3: *Playing at the Curious Kids' Museum in St. Joseph, MI, June 2007*
4: *Banging a drum, June 2007*
5: *Sniffing the daffodils, March 2007*

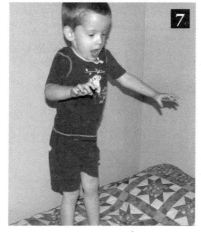

Logan

6: Trying out a big rig, July 2007
7: Breaking in the big boy bed, September 2007
8: "Look at my silly hat!" November 2007
9: Taking a turn at the reins at a wildlife park, September 2007
10: New clothes for Easter 2008

Alex celebrates the first night in his big boy bed.

Chapter 14

Bring On the Big Boy Beds

September 2007

Even though it took the boys a while to get rolling on the bedtime naughtiness, they seem determined to catch up with the girls by dedicated bad behavior. Their blinds now look almost as bad as the girls' set does, and they've figured out how to yank hard on the closet doors to pop off the locks on the top. The boys' crowning moment was when I found a dried up chunk of poo rattling around in an empty dresser drawer that hadn't been opened in months.

One thing I've noticed about having boys and girls the exact same age is that girls do things a lot faster than boys, which is not always a bad thing for the boys. My girls are more demanding, curious and opinionated than their laid-back brothers. The girls tend to whine more and pout for ages, where the boys just give each other a thumping, sniffle a bit and get over it.

It's been about a year and half since the girls started climbing out of their cribs and got switched to big girl beds, with all the chaos and naughtiness that goes with sudden freedom behind closed doors. Because of their tendency to just go with the flow, the boys have remained in their cribs all this time, happy to keep on sleeping there without trying to escape.

Still, they are getting on towards being four, and the cribs were starting to squeak in protest as their weight climbed over 30 pounds, so we decided it was about time that Logan and Alex switched to big beds. Kyle's not so happy with changes, so we decided to save him for later after breaking in the other two.

While we were at it, we decided to buy new mattresses for two of the girls and Connor, who were sleeping on hand-me-down sets almost as old as me. I went to the mattress store, picked out a set that would work and told the clerk I'd like five of them. After she got over her shock, we had the usual discussion that started with "HOW many kids do you have?!" We finished the order and arranged for delivery the next day, some time between 4 and 6 p.m.

The following day, we got the boys' bed frames all set up and laid out their new bedding. Everyone was excited and kept asking when the new beds would be here. I began to wonder myself, as 4, 5 and then 6 p.m. came and went. A few phone calls later, we were assured that it would be 7:30 at the latest, which also came and went.

The kids were tired, so we just decided to get them ready for bed and the mattresses would have to wait downstairs until morning, whenever they arrived. Just as we had all the kids nearly settled in bed, we heard a truck backing into the driveway and the fun began.

New mattresses began rustling up the steps, while old ones went slithering down. The cats and Kyle were all flipping out about the new noises and strangers, and the girls huddled anxiously around me while strange men tromped around in their bedroom. Connor bounced on every free mattress he could find, leaping and howling with joy until he was banished to the guest room so he'd be out of the way. Finally everything was in place, and I began to make up all the new beds with fresh bedding.

Of course, the first order of business was jumping on all the new mattresses to break them in properly. Once we had that out of the way, the girls soon settled down, and we began to work on getting the boys arranged in their new beds.

Logan and Alex had such proud looks on their faces as they climbed in all by themselves, and they oohed and aahed over the new quilts Grandma Betty had made for their beds. They both snuggled right down in their crispy new sheets and let us take the obligatory pictures of them looking so big and brave.

They seemed really enthusiastic at first, but as soon as we tried to turn off the lights and leave them alone in their new beds, the wailing began. After a bit of fussing around, Logan ended up sleeping very nicely in his big boy bed. Although Alex didn't want to be in the new bed, he cried bitterly when we put him in his crib instead, where he eventually fell asleep in between sniffles.

For a few days, we limped along between cribs and beds, until we just pulled the cribs out and forced the boys to get used to the new beds. All things considered, they were much easier to switch over than the girls had been, and they tended to stay in their beds much better, too, at least at first.

Once the novelty of the beds wore off, it took the boys a few days to start misbehaving, but overall, they've been much better than the girls. Thanks to their sisters' bad behavior, we knew exactly what we needed to do to the boys' room before letting them into the big beds: all the furniture was bolted to the walls, the registers were screwed in place, the decorations came down and anything moveable was removed.

Now that we've gotten into a routine with Alex and Logan, we're trying to get our nerve up to switch Kyle over, too. He's fascinated with Alex's bed and the Thomas the Tank Engine sheets, and I've caught him ripping Alex's quilt off and sitting right in the middle of the bed to look at all his favorite characters. I guess I'll have to look for a Thomas sheet set for Kyle's bed, too, and hope he likes it enough to stay in it.

I'm sure it's only a matter of time before the boys start destroying things the way the girls did, but for now we're just enjoying the calm before the storm and trying to ignore the wrestling matches that often break out when they're supposed to be taking naps.

• •

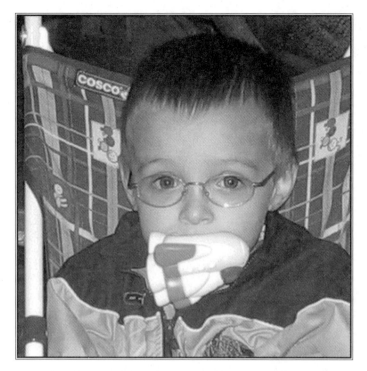

Kyle would rather eat almost anything other than gluten-free crackers!

Chapter 15

So What the Heck is Gluten?

October 2007

We are approaching the one-year mark on the gluten-free diet, and have adjusted pretty well. Kyle still tries to swipe stuff off Logan's plate when he's not looking, which causes Logan to squeal and me to shout, "NO!" loud enough so that Kyle drops the forbidden food out of shock. Poor Kyle probably thinks his middle name is "No, no" or "Drop it" for as many times as I say his name followed by one of those phrases.

If you had asked me what gluten is a few months ago, I'd have said it's something that comes in a squeeze bottle and you use it to stick papers or craft projects together. Gluten is actually a protein found in wheat, barley and rye. The sticky part is pretty accurate, because wheat/gluten is used in many processed foods as a thickener to make things stick together better. It also fouls up the insides of people who can't tolerate wheat, which may be Kyle's latest issue.

For some time, I've been wondering if Kyle might have autism, a developmental disorder that affects communication and socialization. As a parent, it's one of those things that you don't even want to think about since there's no cure. Although there's a lot of information out there on the disorder, the cause and cure for autism seem to be just big question marks at this point.

Our pediatrician recently recommended we take Kyle for an evaluation by a specialist, and the earliest we can get in is January, which seems like an eternity away. I had prayed for something to do to help Kyle in the meantime, since I really don't like just sitting around waiting.

One of my mother-in-law's friends has celiac disease and cannot tolerate gluten in her diet. She had read a lot on the subject and when she found out we were concerned about Kyle and his possible diagnosis, she gave me a book about gluten sensitivity, especially in children with autism. After reading the book and doing more research on my own, I decided to try Kyle on a gluten-free diet with the attitude, "Can't hurt, might help."

The week before we were ready to begin, I copied the lists of acceptable and forbidden ingredients and set out to explore the health food stores and specialty aisles of my regular grocery store. Once I found the gluten-free (GF) stuff, the first thing that hit me was the price: $6 for a box of crackers? $4 for a loaf of bread? $5 for a small box of cereal? Good grief! I had no idea what would taste good or even appeal to Kyle, so I bought a sampling of things to try and bit my tongue when I got the total at the cash register.

While doing the rest of my regular grocery shopping, I started to read almost every label and was amazed at how many things contained some form of wheat. That first shopping trip took me hours longer than usual as I strained my eyes to get through the fine print of ingredient listings, ferreting out the sneaky descriptions that really meant "gluten."

I cleared out a shelf in the pantry for Kyle's things, planned a menu for the first week and held my breath as we began Day One. At breakfast that first day, I pulled out a box of Kyle's GF cereal that had a cute picture of a gorilla on it. What a riot that caused! I had no trouble getting Kyle to eat and enjoy his special new cereal, but I had a very hard time convincing the others that they couldn't have some, too. After a few days of me saying, "This is Kyle's special food," the kids pretty much accepted that Kyle was trying something new and they were going on with their normal food.

The only major problem I had with the others after that first breakfast was the bad attitude I got the next day when I pulled out a package of GF chocolate chip cookies to give to Kyle, while the rest got plain old animal crackers. I learned quickly that I had to buy GF and regular things that looked as much alike as possible, so that no one would feel left out.

Of that first batch of experimental products, some things were pretty good (the cookies, pretzels and cereal) and some were incredibly nasty (the bread and the crackers). I decided early on to taste everything before I gave it to Kyle, and found that if I thought it was gross, chances were pretty good that Kyle would share that opinion and chuck the offending food on the floor.

I started keeping notes of what was good and what wasn't, since it was so costly to buy something and pitch most of it when Kyle hated the taste or texture. We tried four or five brands of pasta before we found a rice version that was pretty close to regular pasta. The heavy, dense GF bread may be a lost cause, as most kinds we've tried would make a better doorstop than a sandwich.

I bought a few GF cookbooks and shared some recipes with the grandmothers, who were happy to bake up some Kyle-safe cookies when they made treats to bring the others. We are incredibly blessed with such supportive families who are as strict in what they give Kyle as I am. I have heard stories from other families who are trying the GF experiment of grandparents undermining the effort by giving regular snacks, or dismissing the whole GF idea as nonsense.

It does take a while to see results in the GF experiment, but so far Kyle seems happier (or at least no more miserable) than before. He still eats and throws with equal fervor, which drives me nuts to watch piles of that expensive food get swept up after every meal.

The kids have just accepted that special food is part of special Kyle, so they don't even protest any more when he gets something different. In fact, they mostly know what he can't have and they're quite vigilant about screaming for me when I don't see that Kyle is trying to take something illegal off Logan's plate.

And so we wait for January, trying new GF recipes and foods every week and fitting this latest wrinkle into our daily routine. In the meantime, if anyone's in the mood for most any variety of GF cracker, I've got a pile of barely opened ones in my pantry that are yours for the asking. We can prop the door open with a loaf of GF bread, as long as you're careful not to stub your toe on it.

• •

Family Time

1: Sophie and Connor, November 2007
2: Lucy and Connor with the kids' art show that covers our kitchen walls. September 2007
3: Alex and Connor, November 2007
4: Sophie, Isabella and Lucy, Halloween 2007
5: The kids are so proud of their first lumpy snowman! February 2008

Family Time

6: Making friends with the leopard at the Akron Zoo, May 2007
7: Craft time, June 2007
8: Isabella and Lucy at the Cincinnati Zoo, October 2007
9: Fascinated by Dora the Explorer, March 2007
10: Mommy and Connor go for a slide, May 2007

*Logan and Lucy are dressed up
for candy collecting.*

Chapter 16

A Sweet and Stinky Halloween

November 2007
Previously published in the *Beacon Journal*

We do love Halloween in our house, but I'm always thankful when I can ship off the bulk of the candy and let our kids come down off their sugar buzz. I know I won't be able to get away with the disappearing candy trick for too much longer, so I'll have to think up another way to keep them from rotting their teeth right out of their heads every October.

Another Halloween has come and gone in my kid-filled house, and I am left with a bit of a sugar buzz and an overwhelming feeling of thankfulness. I'm not so much thankful for the celebrations being over (okay, maybe a little bit), but rather for having seven healthy and growing kids that make holidays a little crazier and a lot more fun. It (almost) makes all the hard work worthwhile now that the kids, at ages 3 and 5, are able to really enjoy and participate in activities, rather than just riding around looking at things from their strollers.

Thankfully, our huge triple strollers have moved on to other families in the past year. Our big kids are very much into walking everywhere on their own now, except for Kyle, our lone hold-out who still likes to ride in a wagon occasionally. The elimination of the strollers solved one of my biggest Halloween dilemmas: how can I get out of helping Keith with another one of his crazy stroller concoctions? My husband has always been really good at coming up with "creative" Halloween decorating and costume ideas that I get the fun of executing.

So, I was very thankful that the boys were finally big enough to start wearing some of older brother Connor's hand-me-down costumes, since there were rumblings from Daddy about making the kids into Star Wars characters, or something equally time-consuming. Alex was thrilled to get the Thomas the Tank Engine outfit, while Logan made a dashing firefighter. Kyle, the shortest of the boys, was still too small to dive into the costume box, so I made him a simple skunk costume out of a black hoodie adorned with felt ears, stripe and tail.

To get extra mileage out of the costumes for Connor and the girls, we practiced some creative pajama usage. For big brother, we bought roomy Batman pajamas and added a mask and a few layers of warm clothes underneath. My mother came to my rescue by making the girls ruffled white flannel nightgowns that turned easily into adorable angel costumes with the addition of wings and gold halos.

As the big night for trick-or-treating approached, I was confident that this would be our easiest, least stressful Halloween yet. We had plenty of family lined up to help, and all the costumes were comfortable and easy to manage. What we didn't count on was the cold, rainy, generally icky weather that soaked our little characters thoroughly before we were even a block into the trick-or-treating.

After about six houses, we decided to go with Plan B: drive to several friends' houses to show off the kids' costumes, instead of fighting with umbrellas and slopping through mud puddles throughout the neighborhood. Ducking out of the cold rain into the dry garage, we piled right in the van without even going back into the house. Off we went, minus the diaper bag. (If this were a movie, I'd cue the foreboding music right about now.)

Arriving at the first house was fine. Our friends Tom and Carla were excited to see the kids, and gave them plenty of hugs and treats. Less thrilled was poor Sandy, the family dog, who ran barking in circles as she was chased by a squealing pack of rabid angels.

About ten minutes into the visit, my highly-trained poo detector went off. "Do you smell something?" I asked Keith, who didn't, of course. Four of our six are now in big-kid underwear, but everyone had worn pull-ups that night as a precaution, so I wasn't too worried right away. I discovered that our little skunk Kyle had decided to add smell effects to match his costume, which seemed like an easy problem to fix, until I realized that all our diapers and wipes were in another zip code. It wasn't too big a pile and Kyle was happily running around, so we thought we could stand the smell for a few more minutes and went on to our second stop.

At the next house, we apologized to our friends Loretta and Mike for our little stinker and the kids dove into boxes of Jeff and Emily's old big kid toys. Kyle was incredibly happy and cuddly and adorable in his costume, but every time one of us hugged him, we'd make a face and say, "Good thing you're so cute, because you sure smell BAD!" I was mentally kicking myself the whole time for being caught unprepared for the mess, especially after checking again and finding that he'd added another deposit, much larger and more pungent, on top of the first small one.

Finally, I had a brainstorm and asked Lucy, our most trustworthy potty girl, if she would mind going to the bathroom and giving her dry pull-up to Kyle to save all of our noses. A nudist at heart, Lucy thought it was pretty fun to go without undies for a while, so she gladly gave up her pull-up, the smelly issue was finally resolved and the evening was saved.

Sunday night was our traditional trip to Boo at the Zoo. Determined not to make the same mistake twice, I made very sure to pack plenty of clean pull-ups and a full package of wipes. I even made Kyle share a seat with the bag in his wagon, as penance for his stinky behavior the previous night.

The weather on Sunday was no warmer, but at least not rainy, so the worst that happened was a few pairs of chilly hands. Many of the normally sleepy animals were up and moving, and the kids oohed and aahed at the big cats walking on the rock walls far above their heads while we traipsed around to the treat stations. By the end, several of the angels were being carried while half asleep, and three kids were jammed into Kyle's wagon with the treat sacks. We'd had no major disasters or meltdowns, so we said silent prayers of thanks and called the weekend a success.

When we rolled back into the garage later, a straggly trio of angels with bent wings and dirty gowns led the way to the house for clean pajamas, one treat from their bags and some much-needed sleep.

After everyone had been tucked away for the night, Keith and I began our own Halloween tradition of sorting out the loot from the weekend. Snacking as we sorted, we saved one small bowl of the kids' favorites for them to spread out over the following days. The bulk of the junk got unloaded on another thankful group: Keith's co-workers, who are amazed every year at the huge amount of candy seven kids can collect in two small outings!

••••••••••••••••••••••••••••••••••••••

Keith slides into a moment of fun at the
Duke Energy Children's Museum in Cincinnati.

Chapter 17

Miraculous Micro Dating

December 2007

Keith and I have learned to make the most of every minute in the day, and that especially includes the rare minutes we get alone. I honestly don't know how we filled the hours before we had kids, and I can't imagine how we'll deal with the silence some day when the house is empty and it's just the two of us bouncing off the walls together.

Before we had kids, Keith and I would spend hours together every day, just hanging out or strolling through stores or walking in the park. We discussed our days in detail and had lots of time for uninterrupted talks about movies, vacations and plans for the future. Then we had the bright idea to add some kids to the mix.

After Connor was born, we pretty much took him everywhere with us. We were always going somewhere, and still had nearly as many conversations as before. Occasionally, we'd leave him with someone and have a real date night, but it wasn't such a big deal to get out alone.

When the sextuplets came into our lives, things changed radically. Suddenly, we were so sleep-deprived that we barely had the strength to walk down the hall, let alone carry on conversations or go out on dates. With so many much-needed helpers always around, our private time shrank to nearly zero.

As the kids got a little older, we began to realize that we had to get away occasionally to preserve our sanity and our relationship. We were fortunate to have plenty of willing volunteers to cover for us while we took in an occasional movie or had a dinner out.

These days, we don't go on very many real dates, but we do manage to grab moments together. These micro dates usually don't last more than five minutes, since that's about how long it takes the kids to notice we're having fun without them. One of our favorite spots for a micro date is at the side window in our kitchen. There's one spot just beside the refrigerator where the kids can't see us from the play room. We can stand there together quietly and eat the last two cookies in the bowl while watching the neighbor's cat stalking squirrels.

Often, when Keith gets home from work and the kids are occupied with a movie, we'll flop on our bed and stare at the ceiling while I tell him funny stories about things the kids said or did during the day. Those micro dates end pretty quickly when kids come to the gate, see our feet sticking off the edge of the bed and demand to be let through so they can get up on the big bed with us.

On days when we can't turn our backs on the kids for even five seconds before a fight breaks out, one of us plays referee while the other one hides in the front room and watches some bad TV while eating ice cream straight out of the carton. After five minutes (or when ice cream brain freeze sets in), we switch spots, handing over the carton and spoon in the doorway.

Occasionally, on nights when I've cooked something the kids hate for supper (usually something with more than two ingredients like—gag—a casserole), they eat their required bite or two and then excuse their still-hungry tummies from the table, knowing full well there will be nothing else until morning. We are determined to work the pickiness out of our little eaters, and Connor has gotten to the point that he will try just about anything because he knows we won't give in and serve something else until he's made a good effort. On those nights when the kitchen is suddenly vacant of kids, Keith and I look at each other down the length of our huge table and say, "Gosh, what a nice, quiet dinner this is!" and enjoy our casserole without having to jump up every ten seconds to get something or wipe up a spill.

On the craziest of days when we barely look at each other in passing, we spend the last moments before falling into an exhausted sleep chatting about the day. Okay, usually it's me yakking and Keith grunting as he's falling asleep and pretending to still listen.

Every once in a while, we still do get out for a real date, but we feel kind of at a loss when we get to the restaurant, and spend most of our time eating quietly and not saying very much at all. And half the time when we do get a night out, we spend it shopping for things we need for the kids since we rarely are in a store together these days.

Still, in spite of all the time we don't spend together anymore, the micro dates we do get are sweet respite from the pressures of raising seven very opinionated little people. In five minutes, we can share a joke, laugh about some rotten thing the kids did, vent about work or in-laws, give each other shoulder rubs, discuss the next day's schedule and just reconnect as the strong team we have to be in order to survive the chaos of daily life.

We have learned to be efficient in many things, including our time together, to make the most of every minute in a day where there are never enough minutes to get everything done. Just like any other couple, we have our up days and our down days, but somehow we always make it through together and can find something to laugh about at the end of the day.

So when people ask me how we do it, or how our relationship has been since having kids, I can honestly say we do it as a team, with a sense of humor and a whole lot of prayer, and our marriage has never been stronger. We joke that we couldn't afford to leave each other even if we wanted to, so we might as well make the best of it, one micro date at a time!

• •

Mommy and Kyle have a silly moment.
Photo courtesy of The Picture People.

Chapter 18

The Awful "A" Word

January 2008
Previously published in the *Beacon Journal*

Every day since Kyle's autism diagnosis has been a mixture of emotions. Some days I'm hopeful and confident that we can help him have a normal life. On other days, I'm worried about who will care for him when we're gone. Usually the hopeful emotions win, but our story is one that is repeated too many times throughout the country as thousands of new autism cases are diagnosed every year. My hope for this chapter is that after reading it, you can understand a bit more about this growing epidemic and the struggles that families with autistic children face every day.

I don't know exactly when I began to suspect that my son Kyle had autism. As the third born of my sextuplets, he had an uphill battle from birth, right along with his brothers and sisters. Each one of them stayed in the Neonatal Intensive Care Unit (NICU) at Akron Children's Hospital for nearly two months after being born 12 weeks prematurely. Each one of them struggled to learn to breathe on their own and drink from a bottle. Each one of them was a miracle for even surviving to be born in the first place.

At the beginning, when the kids all came home from the hospital, the days were a blur of feedings, diapers and the unrelenting demands of caring for six preemies with the help of a huge corps of volunteers. There was very little time to worry about when each child hit all the usual baby milestones like rolling over, sitting up, crawling, walking and talking. It just seemed that they did each new thing one right after the other. Except for Kyle.

Kyle took the longest to get the hang of bottle feeding in the NICU. He was the last to roll, to sit and to crawl. We thought he'd never walk, since he kept right on crawling for at least six months after everyone else had taken off on their own two feet. He was happy and healthy and ate like a little diapered pig, so we tried not to compare him too much to the others.

At some point, I began seeing lists of the warning signs of autism popping up everywhere. They were in parenting magazines. They were in the newspapers and on the web. I even found one on a box of cereal. Every time I found a new list, I would read them and mentally compare them to Kyle: doesn't talk or babble (check), interested in spinning objects like ceiling fans (check), makes little eye contact (check), doesn't respond when his name is called (check), does not interact much with other children (check), has repetitive behaviors like jumping on his toes and flapping his hands (double check), does not react well to changes in routine (big check)...

The lists went on and on, but I always dismissed autism as soon as I got to the item about most autistic children not liking to be cuddled or held. Kyle was a cuddle bug from the very first day. He was the first baby I got to hold 24 hours after their birth. He has always loved to be hugged, tickled and wrestled with, and was generally a very happy baby.

Gradually, as Kyle got older and passed his second birthday, our pediatrician began to voice his concerns about why Kyle wasn't talking, and asked if we wanted to have him evaluated for speech or hearing problems. We had Kyle's hearing tested and found it normal in spite of repeated ear infections. We dismissed the doctor's questions about Kyle not talking because he'd been so late to do everything else. It just took him longer, but he'd get there eventually, I reasoned.

You may think that I merely had my head in the sand at this point, but life was busy with so many little ones to watch over, and time slid quickly by. Keith and I tried not to worry too much about Kyle's issues, and almost unconsciously learned to cope with the things that sent him into tantrums or hysterical screaming fits. He couldn't tolerate drumming or clapping, and church services on Sunday were always interrupted by Kyle's wailing if we suddenly began singing or applauding when he wasn't expecting it. Strangers and changes in routine also had the potential to send Kyle into orbit, so we tried to carefully guard him and prepare him for new experiences ahead of time.

Before I knew it, it was time for Kyle's third year check-up, and the pediatrician again mentioned that Kyle's lack of speech was concerning. Kyle had actually said a word or two just before that, so I used those examples to convince the doctor that more time was needed for Kyle to catch on. Plus, he had just begun preschool, and I wanted to give his new speech therapist a chance to see what she could do with Kyle.

Last May I wrote a column (Chapter 8 in this book) about how I spent my Mother's Day. I had previously talked about Kyle jumping, squealing and flapping in front of the TV, and wrote then how he preferred to sit quietly with me rather than run around in the yard with his siblings. A few days later, a kind reader emailed me a very tactful suggestion that Kyle had autism. She mentioned that she worked with autistic children and asked if we'd ever had Kyle evaluated for the disorder. At the time, I was still heavily in denial about the whole thing, hoping he'd magically start talking one day and I wouldn't have to face my growing fears that something was deeply wrong. I responded politely but firmly and pretty much told her to butt out, as I'm sure she expected I might do. But she had planted a mental seed that just would not go away, and I am thankful now for her kind words.

I began to read about autism, and allowed myself for the first time to consider what life might be like if what I feared was actually confirmed. I prayed a lot, and quietly discussed autism with Keith, sharing what I'd read in the brief minutes before we fell into our typical exhausted sleep. I began to watch Kyle carefully and compare him more closely to the children I was reading about. I found out that although there is much that can be done to help a child with autism, there is no cure for the disorder that affects communication and social skills. Autism began to seem like a very real and very frightening possibility.

In August, after taking one of the other kids to the pediatrician for some crud they had, we began to discuss Kyle again and the doctor finally insisted that I take Kyle back to Akron Children's Hospital to be fully evaluated. Neither of us said "autism" during that conversation, but I know both of us were thinking it.

Phone calls were made, many lengthy questionnaires and medical histories were filled out and we began the nearly five month-long wait until a specialist could see and evaluate Kyle. Not being one to just sit around and wait happily, I began looking into ways we could try to help Kyle in the meantime.

As I mentioned in Chapter 15, a friend gave me a book on gluten (wheat) sensitivity in autistic children, which opened my eyes to lots of other physical problems Kyle was having, like failure to gain weight and increased fussiness after eating. After much research, we made the leap and put Kyle on a strict gluten-free diet. At first I felt like the proverbial Wicked Witch, denying him foods he loved like macaroni, pretzels, crackers and pizza, but with a little trial and error we found decent substitutes for most of his favorites. It wasn't very hard to get Kyle to eat those darned expensive substitutes since he will eat pretty much anything; the real challenge was in convincing his brothers and sisters why they didn't need "special food" too!

About a week after beginning the gluten-free diet, I witnessed a small miracle: Kyle looked at himself in a mirror for the first time in his life. This may not sound like much, but for a boy who never once, even as a baby, had the slightest bit of interest in his own reflection, this was HUGE. He began running (another thing he almost never did) back and forth to the bathroom just to look at himself dozens of times a day.

He began to smile and laugh more, and the perpetual worried wrinkle he wore on his forehead disappeared somewhere in week two of the diet. And over the course of three months, he gained six pounds and finally got tall enough to move out of the 2T pants he'd been wearing for a year and a half.

As chief diaper changer, I noticed that the gritty, sandy mess that had filled Kyle's diaper for years soon disappeared and was replaced with normal stool, which also thrilled me way more than you would believe. We tried excluding dairy from Kyle's diet, too, but didn't really see any improvement from that like we had with eliminating gluten, so after a two-month trial, we phased some dairy back in.

The most positive and exciting change was in Kyle's demeanor. He slowly became more tolerant of noise, crowds and schedule changes, and finally got to the point where he could sit in church again without throwing a fit and trying to get away. Kyle began to make more eye contact with us and with his teachers, who reported slow but steady progress every week. He even would turn occasionally when we'd call his name. Once in a while, we'd swear we heard a word, but he would never repeat it when asked, so we were always left wondering.

At a suggestion from our pediatrician, we added fish oil supplements to Kyle's routine. I'd read that fish oil helps the parts of the brain that control concentration, memory and language, so we thought it was worth the experiment. The first day, I fought with him to get a dribble of oil into his mouth and didn't mention it to Kyle's teacher at school. She brought him out at the end of the session and raved about his excellent concentration and how he had really attended to all the tasks she'd asked him to try. The second day, after another round of fish oil, his speech therapist walked him out and was beaming as she told me she'd just had the best speech session ever with Kyle where he picked his own picture when asked, a first for him. So the fish oil became a permanent addition to Kyle's diet.

To help his language development, Kyle's teachers gave him a button that said, "More!" when he pressed it. The other kids thought it was hilarious to see him beating away on that button at the table, and then watch me scramble to see what it was that he wanted "more" of. One morning, after I'd just refilled his cereal and was on the floor mopping up someone else's milk spill, I heard the thwackity-thwack of Kyle hitting his button.

"More! More!" said the button. "Just a minute!" I said, still wiping. "More! More!" repeated the button. "Hang on! Almost done!" I said again. "More! More!" the button insisted. "All RIGHT, Kyle! I hear you!" I finally growled in my least patient tone, and then promptly started laughing at the stupidity of what I'd said. Here I was trying to teach the poor kid to talk, then chewing him out when he was banging away at the button and talking in the only way he knew how. So I got him "More! More!" tasty gluten-free cereal and mentally kicked myself for a few minutes.

Keith and I were impatient for the holidays to come and go so we could get to January and the appointment at Children's Hospital. Finally the big day arrived. We said a lot of prayers, packed up our bag of treats and toys for Kyle and headed off to confirm the news we already knew in our hearts.

Kyle performed like a champ, demonstrating the skills and quirks that we were so familiar with, but had been afraid he'd be too anxious to show a stranger. After several hours of observation, discussion and interacting with Kyle, the doctor told us that our suspicions were correct, and our son did have autism. She said we were already doing good things for him by having him in a therapy-intensive preschool, putting him on a special diet and giving him the supplements. We took a deep breath, looked at each other and said, "So what do we do next?"

Kyle, worn out by an afternoon of challenges, pulled his favorite pink chenille blanket over his head and fell asleep in the corner as we discussed various therapies and additional tests with the doctor. The doctor said we had to begin pushing Kyle harder to communicate. She also suggested teaching him simple sign language so he would have a way of talking until real words came. Kyle was still snoring as we carried him to the lab for a blood test, but quickly woke up in full scream when we held him down so the technician could draw two very large vials of blood.

Although we both seemed matter-of-fact about the diagnosis the day we got it, it took Keith and me several days to really come to grips with the situation. I was 99% sure Kyle had autism before we went in, but there was a big mental leap required to handle that last 1% where near-certainty becomes reality. In the end, both of us said a prayer of thanks that we weren't facing much worse, and decided to get on with the work ahead.

I began showing Kyle basic signs, which he thinks are hilarious for some reason. Last weekend, I was working on the signs for "mommy" and "daddy" and getting nothing but giggles out of him. The other kids got into the act, too, and pretty soon the entire table was full of little hands enthusiastically signing "mommy," "daddy" and "thank you" while Kyle laughed and laughed.

I was pretty sure he was just messing with me and not paying attention, until Sunday morning when he came down the stairs and into the kitchen to greet me. I looked down and said hello to him, then watched in amazement as he deliberately put his thumb on his chin in the sign for "mommy" before popping that thumb into his mouth and marching away without any idea what a big deal it was.

I have no idea where this new road is going to lead our family. We are by no means autism experts and are looking for answers just like any other family that has been touched by this disorder. I know we will have setbacks and miracles every day, and we'll just have to deal with them as best we can, with lots of prayer and plenty of faith and hard work. We have only begun to explore what this diagnosis means for Kyle and for his siblings, who have all wondered when he will begin to talk.

Lucy asked me recently, "Is Kyle a baby?" I explained that Kyle is not a baby, but he doesn't talk yet because his brain works differently than everyone else's does. Big brother Connor was listening intently and said, "I can't wait to hear what Kyle's voice sounds like!" I just smiled and said, "I know it will be beautiful!"

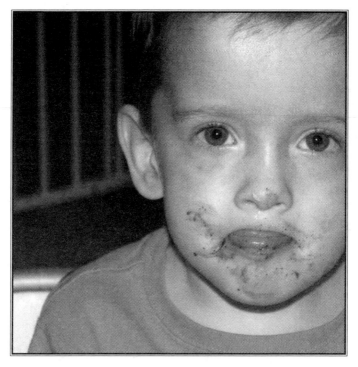

Logan has always been my dirty-faced,
stubborn angel.

Chapter 19

A Logan Moment in the Bathroom

February 2008

I am still struggling with Logan's potty training, but I know it's just a matter of finding the right motivation. He'd probably be embarrassed to go on a date with a Pull-Up on, so I guess I just have to wait him out. I keep watching for signs that he's finally ready, but some days it feels like I'll still be buying him training pants with my Social Security check.

I consider myself a smart mom. I have figured out how to manage seven kids, four cats, a hard-working husband and a busy household and make sure most things get done when they need to. Everyone always has clean clothes, a (mostly) clean home and something nutritious to eat. (Whether or not they actually eat it is up to them.) I manage 1,001 details every day and still find a moment or two for myself.

So if I'm so darn smart and efficient and full of wonderful skills, why in the world can't I figure out how to get an almost-4-year-old to go on the potty? This is the question that haunted me while trying not to rip out my own or Logan's hair last week after yet another disastrous potty attempt.

I have successfully potty-trained five other kids and am down to my final two. Kyle will be a while before he's ready, so I've been concentrating my efforts on Logan, my smiling devil of a boy. This is the kid that can kick his sister down the stairs, fully knowing I just saw him do it, and then deny he did it with a sickeningly sweet smile on his angelic face.

I have tried every single tactic that worked with the first five children: bribery, reading books, giving treats, singing songs, putting them in underwear and just letting them pee until they learn, leaving them alone on the potty until they're so bored they just give up and go… but none of these methods has made the slightest dent in Logan's potty armor. I tried a year ago when I trained Alex, thinking Alex would be a good influence on Logan. Alex got it, but Logan didn't, so I decided to wait a bit and try again. In my second attempt, I have faithfully put him on the potty every day for the past three months with zero success.

Logan just flat-out refuses to go on the potty. He is a pro at all the other parts: pulling pants up and down, sitting patiently, washing hands and even turning off the light. He just misses that one crucial step.

So on that fateful day last week, lunch was just wrapping up when I smelled that tell-tale smell on the boys side of the table. When I discovered it was coming from Logan and that his pants were still empty,

I said, "Great! You can sit and poop on the potty, since I can tell you have to go!" He was enthusiastic and willingly went to sit.

I decided to let him sit there until I'd cleaned up the kitchen. Fifteen minutes later, still nothing. So I emptied the dishwasher, too. Still nothing. I put in a load of laundry. Nothing. Finally when we hit the 30-minute mark, I figured his feet and butt cheeks had gone to sleep, so I'd better let him get up.

He cheerfully pulled up his pants, flushed his non-existent poop, and climbed the step stool to wash his hands. Somewhere in those 30 seconds, he pooped in his Pull-Up. I don't think there is a mother in the land that would fault me for having wrung his neck right there. Maybe we'll get it by the time he goes to kindergarten.

• •

Family Time

1: Mommy and the kids visit the Oscar Mayer Weinermobile and its driver at the local grocery store. November 2006

2: Daddy and Kyle, June 2007

3: Lucy & Daddy make friends with a baby duck at the petting zoo, September 2007

4: Lucy, Connor, Sophie, Mommy, Isabella, Logan, Daddy, Kyle and Alex, Easter 2008

Family Time

6: Connor reads a scary dinosaur book to the girls, December 2007

7: There was barely a daffodil left in the yard when these kids were done picking! April 2008

8: Isabella, Lucy, Sophie and Connor ready for the first day of school, August 2007

9: Playing with the safari animals at the sextuplets' 4th birthday party, February 2008

10: Daddy, Kyle, Connor, Lucy, Logan, Sophie, Isabella, Alex and Grandpa Bud at the
     Cleveland Metroparks Zoo, August 2007

We collapse after the big birthday party.
From left: Alex, Mommy, Kyle, Connor,
Lucy, Isabella, Daddy, Sophie and Logan.
Photo courtesy of Steve Tirrell of Andy's Parties

Chapter 20

Jerry Springer Throws a Party

February 2008

With apologies to Andy's Parties, the sextuplets' fourth birthday party really did seem like something the TV host could have set up. Thankfully, all the kids and most of the adults were oblivious to the drama, so at least the whole event looked like a regular party to 97% of the people there. As I often say, our lives are never boring or quiet.

The story I want to tell you about my kids' fourth birthday party is the exact one I can't quite tell you. It's so ridiculous, so typical of how my life works out that you would barely believe it even if I broke a promise and told you all the gruesome details.

Let me begin at the beginning. I have always liked birthday parties. What's not to like? Cake, ice cream, presents, family and friends....all my favorite things. Since having kids, one of my new favorite things is seeing what a big kick they get out of birthdays. They love the extra attention and the oddball cakes I make that require a little imagination to see what they're supposed to be. And of course, they love the presents.

Our house is full of plenty of noise and chaos on a daily basis, so when big occasions roll around, we try to keep things fairly calm. We had never done a true kids' party for any of our children. The thought of having any more kids in my house than the seven that belong here always gave me the heebie-jeebies, so we usually just did low-fuss family parties with grandparents, aunts, uncles and close friends.

However, this year a very generous (and brave) man named Steve from Andy's Parties offered to donate a safari-themed party for the kids and up to 15 friends. The service included set up, clean up, activities, decorating and food, so after debating briefly about it, Keith and I decided, "What the heck?" and sent out invitations to all their little preschool classmates (and a few older friends for Connor).

We had no idea what to expect. When I was a kid (geez, do I sound old now!), we celebrated with just immediate family and it was a very low-key occasion. The birthday kid got to pick the main course and what kind of cake they wanted, and that was about all. There were a few presents, we celebrated the occasion and we called it a day.

Today's kids' parties are quite a bit more involved than that, apparently. Steve showed up with a van as big as ours, only his was full of helpers and supplies, not seven car seats. Each helper carried a humongous stuffed safari animal, the kind you see in the store and wonder, "Who would want a stuffed lion bigger than their child?" The kids loved them right away, and began jumping on the animals (and each other) while the helpers rearranged our kitchen, set up the activities and brought in countless loads of supplies.

I felt kind of guilty for just standing back and watching the crew work, but that was part of the deal, so I settled for making sure my kids weren't killing each other in the safari wrestling pit.

The little guests began arriving in ones and twos and immediately dove right into activities as my kids squealed with delight when their school friends kept appearing. The party crew kept things moving smoothly and kept everyone happy, except for Kyle, who decided pretty quickly that he'd be happiest in another room with Daddy and a movie.

The pizza appeared and vanished quickly, as did the cake and ice cream. The moms were hanging out talking in the kitchen and I was feeling pretty good about how our first kids' party was turning out. And that's when it happened—that part of the story that I just can't tell you much about.

I have never had a good poker face. I would love to have seen my expression when one of the moms (who I had only just met an hour before) felt the need to lean in close, swear me to secrecy and air her family's dirty laundry. The abbreviated version is that there was an ugly, painful affair which resulted in half-siblings (and their mothers who hate each other) that coincidentally ended up at the same party. Our party, of course.

Although there was no way I could have known or prevented the fateful meeting, I was still horrified and embarrassed. I was wishing for it all to be the kind of joke where the hidden camera pops out at the end, or for Jerry Springer to just swoop in and take the whole crazy love triangle with him, or for the floor to crack open and drop me into the basement. None of those things happened, so I just had to stand there with a dazed look on my face and wait for the party to mercifully come to an end.

The kids, all 20 of them, had a great time playing games, dancing and trying out their new safari helmets and binoculars. Amazingly, it was my kids who turned out to be the shy ones of the bunch, taking turns hugging me when the noise got to be too much. But in the end, they all said they had a great time, so we called the whole thing a success.

As the guests filed out and the party crew began their clean-up, I just had to shake my head and laugh as I told Keith my too-awful-to-be-true story.

"Typical!" he said. "We can't even pull off a normal kids' party without some kind of drama!"

The party planners snapped a couple of pictures of our exhausted family to commemorate the occasion (as if we could forget this party any time soon!) and left with our profound thanks.

As we replaced the furniture and prepared for the family party the following day, I took comfort in knowing that at least the second party was only filled with the nutty people we already knew. I was looking forward to it. After all, I had a great story I could almost share with them.

• •

Connor loves them, but I can't even tell you how many K'nex building pieces I've pulled from under couches, down registers or inside Kyle's mouth and tucked into my pocket until I happen to be in Connor's room and can empty out my stash.

Chapter 21

Poking Around in My Pockets

February 2008

If you think my pockets are full, you should see the collection of junk I carry in my purse now. I used to be able to get away with smaller, cuter purses, but now I just give up and buy a large backpack-style purse so I can have my hands free while carrying my first aid supplies, headache pills, toy cars, Barbie brushes, coupon organizer and always-empty wallet.

Since becoming a mom, my pockets are constantly full of interesting and disgusting bits of things that I pick up off the floor and tuck away. If you were to catalog the contents of my pockets, you would get a pretty accurate picture of where my kids are at in their development.

For example, when my kids were very small, my pockets were mostly full of used tissues or napkins spattered with the remnants of spit-up or the latest round of colds. When they got a little bigger, one pocket held dirty pacifiers and the other had clean ones. (The trick was remembering which pocket was which).

When the kids got to be more mobile, my pockets filled up with tiny things like rocks, tires off Connor's cars, dead bugs, fingernail clippings and any other disgusting little piece of crud I'd found on the carpet and didn't want them to put in their mouths.

After we hit the table food stage, my pockets began to house things like Cheerios or dried-up pieces of macaroni and cheese that I found sticking to their clothes after mealtime.

Presently, we are still struggling with Kyle putting all kinds of junk in his mouth, so my pockets are always full of spit-covered things I've taken from him. I have him well-trained so that when I yell, "Spit!" and put my hand under his chin, he ejects a Barbie shoe, hair clip, Polly Pocket dress, bouncy ball, Lego block, rock, used Band-Aid or a spitball made from the corner of a book he's been chewing on. My pockets get emptied frequently and the things that are worth saving go into a bowl on top of the refrigerator full of Kyle-tasted objects that are still worth playing with when he finally gets past the puppy stage.

On an almost hourly basis, my pockets become landfills overflowing with Band-Aid wrappers, bits of crayon, discarded stickers, dryer sheets, torn corners of book pages and crumpled reminder notes, all waiting to be scooped out the next time I pass a trash can.

It's a small dream, but I look forward to the day when I can put my hands in my pockets without flinching or doing a quick mental check to see what I might be touching.

Sophie says,
"I can't help it if I have a good imagination!"

Chapter 22

A Scrap of Quiet Time

April 2008

Every once in a while, Quiet Time really is quiet, but I get nervous when it's too quiet upstairs. Like any good mom, my radar goes off and I have to check things out when there's a sudden drop in the noise level. That's what convinces my kids that I have "magic ears," as Connor calls them. I've also got them believing that I have an extra eye on the back of my head under my hair.

Imagination is a wonderful thing. Throughout the centuries, dreamers with great imaginations have been responsible for countless inventions, innovations and masterpieces. In 4-year-old hands, though, the power of imagination is a dangerous weapon, and when you put three 4-year-olds together, the possibilities for naughtiness are infinite.

Connor stopped napping ages ago, and the sextuplets have also decided to go nap-free in recent months. However, I am not ready to give up that precious hour of quiet time after lunch, where I get to eat my own lunch in peace, read a chapter of a book, check email and generally recharge for the second half of the day. So I instituted Quiet Time, where the kids have to spend an hour playing quietly in their rooms after lunch.

I hoped by calling it "Quiet Time," I would inspire them to do something crazy, like, oh, maybe BE QUIET. Not so much. In spite of my personal resolve to yell less (since it does no good anyhow), I find myself running up and down the stairs several times during that hour, scolding everyone back to bed, breaking up fights and checking on why I've heard the water running in the bathroom for 10 minutes.

The kids haven't quite caught on to the fact that when they jump off their beds or scoot the stool across the bathroom floor, I can actually hear it downstairs. The looks of astonishment on their faces when I whip open the door and catch them out of their beds and doing something naughty are always pretty funny.

Much less funny are the things I've actually found them doing when they're supposed to be resting and playing quietly. The boys mostly just wrestle or yank all the covers off their beds to make a big nest in the middle of their floor, but the girls are the hands-down champs of thinking up rotten things to do.

It doesn't help that the girls have access to the bathroom during Quiet Time, just in case they actually want to use the toilet for its proper function. One afternoon, Isabella and Sophie decided that after peeing in the toilet, they would try it out as a wading pool, too. They must've found it hard to stand up in, because by the time I found them, there was a great deal of yellow water all over the bathroom floor and counters, while the culprits were wet past their knees. Lucy was very quick to point out that she hadn't helped and had only stood in the bathroom doorway and watched.

The bathroom sinks are also very attractive to over-active imaginations. One day when quiet time was over, I came in to find the girls with wet hair, but only around their faces. Lucy finally confessed that they'd been playing puppy and getting drinks out of the faucet, lapping it up with their tongues and dragging their hair in the water in the process.

And they quickly discovered that the big cupboards under the sinks were nearly empty and made great hidey-holes to curl up inside with toys and blankets. One harder thing to figure out was why toys that get flushed down the toilet don't ever come back.

It's been very educational for me to clean up after these imagination sessions, and I've learned many things I never knew before having little girls. For example, did you know that Chap-stick makes a great marker for writing on walls and mirrors, and dries in stiff points when you put it in your hair? I bet you never imagined how easy it is to rip vinyl blinds into segments and shove them into the nearest register, or that you can fit almost half a blind in said register before the slats start poking out the top instead of going down the vent. And I'm sure you've never heard that the best use for a stolen memo pad is to rip off each individual sheet and shove it in the other register until it's completely blocked, so no heat gets into the room at all.

Once in a great while, the girls actually take a nap, but rarely in bed. I've found Bella, crashed out after some especially tiring bad behavior, sprawled in the chair asleep, or tucked under Sophie's bed (which gave me a moment of panic until I heard her snoring).

After all this, you might wonder why I even bother with Quiet Time any more. I'm pretty sure stupidity and desperation are right at the top of the list of reasons. In my long days, I get very few moments of down time, so when it's Quiet Time, I put a load of clothes in the dryer to mask some of the stomping around upstairs and try to reassemble my strength and sanity for the rest of the day. In spite of the mess, I find it's totally necessary for the kids and me to have a break from each other.

On good days, I get enough strength back to make it until 8:00 p.m. On bad days, we head up to bed at 7:00 and call the game early on account of bad behavior. Then Keith and I sit downstairs, enjoy the silence and imagine how empty our lives would be without our creative bunch of mischief-makers.

"Please, can I get a monkey?
Pleeeeeeeease?"

Chapter 23

Monkey Madness

May 2008

My kids are masters of persuasion and can think up almost plausible reasons why they need the latest toy or fancy tennis shoe. I'm practicing saying, "No, you don't really need it," in my firmest tone so I'm ready for the teenage years.

Connor is a television advertiser's dream. He remembers and repeats any commercials he sees during the few cartoons he watches. I try to limit the kids' exposure to TV with commercials and just stick to DVDs because they get the "gimmies" after watching a few minutes of Dora or Diego on Nick Jr.

One day last month, Connor watched an ad for some kind of incredible expanding purse with all these pockets, then came out to the kitchen and told me why I needed the purse and all the features it had. The next day, I was digging for something in my boring, non-expandable purse, and he said, "I bet you wish you had that expanding purse, huh?"

And he almost talked Keith into ordering me these fancy blown-glass bulbs that are automatic houseplant watering devices. Never mind the fact that I have a grand total of one houseplant, a pitifully tiny African violet that only has enough strength to bloom once a year and is smaller than the glass bulb watering tool.

When Connor asked me a few days ago if we could go to Chuck E. Cheese's, I knew it wasn't from past experience, since I can't stand the place and refuse to take my kids there (mean mom, I know). "Why do you want to go to Chuck E. Cheese's?" I asked. "Because that's where a kid can be a kid!" he said in a "Well, duh!" tone of voice. So I shouldn't have been at all surprised at the way the day began.

"Good morning, Mom!" yelled Connor this morning as he whipped open the bathroom door and marched in. "Can I get a monkey as a pet?"

Usually I'm feeling relatively sharp and ready to go after I've had my morning shower, so I was pretty sure I must have just misunderstood Connor.

"Um, what?" I managed.

"A monkey," he repeated. "As a pet. I want one."

"Where on earth did you get that idea?" I asked.

"On TV," he said in a matter-of-fact tone.

"There is no way we're getting a pet monkey!" I sputtered.

Out went the lower lip, down went the eyebrows and the arms folded across his narrow chest in the typical mad pose.

114

"Why not?" Connor demanded.

"Well, a monkey's a lot of work, kind of like having another baby. Monkeys have to wear diapers so they don't poop everywhere. Do you want to change poopy monkey diapers?" I asked, forgetting that angry six-year-olds are completely immune to reason and good sense. "Humph!" he said. "I still want one!"

And then, beginning with the classic words my own mother had used on many occasions in my own childhood, I said firmly, "Well, when you're a grown up and you have your own house, you can do whatever you like. But in my house, there will be no pet monkeys. EVER."

"Fine!" he snarled, and flung himself dramatically on my bed, pulling the blankets over his head. In a slightly muffled tone, he declared, "I'm not getting out of this bed until you say you'll buy me a monkey!"

Until then, I had been doing a good job of keeping a straight face, but that was the last straw. I finally burst out laughing, which really helped the situation, as you might imagine.

"I mean it!" he howled with the covers still over his head.

It was too good not to share with Keith, who leaves for work at 6 a.m. and is lucky enough to miss these touching little early-morning moments. So I called him and put on my best mock-serious tone.

"We have a major problem," I said.

"Uh oh, what now?" he said, preparing for the worst.

"Connor says he wants a pet monkey, and he's refusing to get out of your side of the bed until I say he can have one."

There was snickering on the other end.

"And he says he's serious!" More snickering.

When I hung up, Connor roared, "Fine! Then I'm not getting you a Christmas present!" He rolled out of bed and stomped away upstairs.

I expected the monkey madness to pass quickly, but Connor hung onto his mad face for a good hour, until it was almost time to go to school. The rest of the day was pretty quiet and I thought he must have forgotten all about his big idea, until just before supper.

I was tossing out a bag of trash and Connor ran up behind me and hugged me enthusiastically. "I love you, Mommy!"

"Thank you, honey!" I said, returning the hug.

In the next breath, he said, "Why can't I get a monkey?"

I'm mentally preparing myself to get a lump of coal in my stocking this December.

• •

Our doormat says it all.

Chapter 24

The Road Ahead

And so I have run out of stories for the moment, but I know another adventure is right around the corner for this family. We try not to look too far into the future since some scary things are waiting there (braces, glasses, driving, dating…eeek!), but instead focus on the next few months.

Connor will begin first grade soon and the kids have one year left of preschool before they join him at the "big kid school." I know it will be a challenging transition, but it's just one more curve in the road ahead.

A few curves from now, we'll be adding an autism service dog from 4 Paws for Ability to our family, which will be much like adding another child (only without the new stretch marks). The dog will be specially trained to keep Kyle calm and safe and can distract him from his repetitive behaviors. Kyle will be tethered to the dog when we're away from home, which will keep him from bolting for the exit when he's scared. I'm hoping that having people come up and talk to Kyle about his dog will also help with his social and language skills, since he tends to retreat into his own silent little world. I've heard lots of great stories about autism service dogs and the wonderful changes they produce in kids, so I'm hoping for the same thing for Kyle.

All the kids grow and change every day, becoming more like little people rather than the babies I still sometimes call them out of long years of habit. Our lives are never dull and rarely quiet. There's never enough money or time. The work of running this busy household is staggering. And yet there's nothing else I'd rather be doing, except on those occasional really trying days where a deserted island sounds mighty nice.

I don't know what waits around the next bend in the road, so I guess I'll buckle my seat belt and hang on tight for the ride of my life.

Thanks for sharing a few curves in the road with me!

● ●

Acknowledgments

*Writing books and raising children are both team efforts,
so I would like to thank these members of my team,
without whom I would still be staring at a blank computer screen
with hungry kids screaming in the background:*

- My publisher/editor Bernadette Kolar, for taking a chance again and helping me all along the road.
- Betsy Lammerding of the *Beacon Journal*, for being so easy to work with and giving me the chance to share my stories.
- Our parents, Duane and Betty Hofstetter and Bud and Nancy Hanselman, for listening ears, good advice and your unconditional love and support.
- Pastor Michael Swab and the members of Twin Falls United Methodist Church, for all your love, support and prayers from the very beginning. Your kindness means more than you'll ever know!
- My on-call grandmas: Ann Bell, Louise Nichols, Jeannie McGaughey, Donna Poulson, Mae Peck, Joanne "Jojo" Ellison and Jana Poulson, for stopping by for playtime any time I call.
- Our hilarious and supportive friends Loretta, Mike, Emily and Jeff Dempster, Gayle Norris, Dawn and Duane Woodford and all the others who keep us laughing, allow us to vent and cover for us so we can run away when we need to.
- Our extended families, who still pray for and encourage us as they have since the beginning.

- Judy Foguth of Judy's Shear Artistry who continues to snip with love whenever we need her, and who has graciously put up with the crazy friends I've brought to her chair over the years.
- Sharon Incorvati, for going far, far above and beyond all expectations to design the heck out of this book on ridiculously short notice. I owe you about 50 Chinese dinners, my friend!
- Photographer Lori Campbell and her assistants Michelle Parsons and Jami Phillips of The Picture People for magically turning a pack of unruly kids into a cute cover shot.

And saving the best for last, my deepest love, affection
and gratitude goes to my husband and best friend, Keith,
for putting up with me for 12 years, believing that he'll someday
be able to retire and live off my book royalties,
and rolling out of bed every morning
to do the work that keeps our family going
until I hit the bestseller list.

About the Author

Jennifer Hanselman is the mother of Ohio's first set of sextuplets and their energetic big brother. She is married to Keith, her college sweetheart, and lives in Cuyahoga Falls, Ohio. This is her second book, which was written in 15-minute intervals between potty accidents and playroom fights. She has been changing diapers for seven years straight and dreams of the day she can skip the diaper aisle for good.